The Joy of Chocolate

Recipes and Stories from the Wonderful World of the Cacao Bean

PAUL A. YOUNG

KYLE BOOKS

I would like to dedicate this book to my mum Val and
stepfather Kevin, for all their love and support, and to my
loving and supportive partner Luke, and to Kate and Adam,
who always bring light and joy into my life.

An Hachette UK Company
www.hachette.co.uk

First published in Great Britain in 2022 by
Kyle Books, an imprint of Octopus Publishing
Group Limited

Carmelite House
50 Victoria Embankment
London EC4Y 0DZ
www.kylebooks.co.uk

ISBN: 9780857839909

Distributed in the US by Hachette Book Group,
1290 Avenue of the Americas,
4th and 5th Floors, New York, NY 10104

Distributed in Canada by
Canadian Manda Group, 664 Annette Street,
Toronto, Ontario, Canada, M6S 2C8

A Cataloguing in Publication record for this title
is available from the British Library

Printed and bound in China

10 9 8 7 6 5 4 3 2 1

Publishing Director: Judith Hannam
Publisher: Joanna Copestick
Senior Commissioning Editor: Louise McKeever
Text Design: Clare Skeats
Photography: Louise Hagger
Food Stylist: Saskia Sidey
Prop Stylist: Jennifer Kay
Production: Lisa Pinnell

Picture Credits
11 Moritz Wolf/ImageBroker/Alamy Stock Photo
15 Caio Pederneiras/Shutterstock
20 SAABI/Anadolu Agency via Getty Images
23 Courtesy Guittard Chocolate Company
37 Courtesy Paul Young
43 Design and development: Valrhona
© 05/2021 - en _31922 Reproduction
prohibited, all rights reserved
56 Courtesy Grenada Chocolate Company
57 Courtesy Dandelion Chocolate
79 Retro AdArchives/Alamy Stock Photo
80 f8 archive/Alamy Stock Photo
119 United Archives GmbH/Paramount
Pictures/Alamy Stock Photo,
123 From *Chocolat* by Joanne Harris
published by Doubleday. Copyright
©Joanne Harris 1999. Reprinted by
permission of Penguin Books Ltd. ©
129 Photographer Luke Evans,
147 Moritz Klingenstein/Alamy Stock Photo,
Jacket Adobe Stock, 488394428

All other photography is by Louise Hagger
for Kyle Books

Text Credits
21-22 © ICCO, 2022
54 © Phil Landers, 2022
123 © Joanne Harris,
www.joanne-harris.co.uk, 2022
128-29 © Prudence Stait, 2022
145-46 © Tijen, 2022
148-49 © Kate Johns, 2022

❧ Contents ❧

Introduction

Every time you or I buy or choose chocolate, it's a deeply emotional decision. It's not a quick or flimsy purchase, but a considered and complex choice that starts way before you make the journey to the shop. What is it about chocolate that makes it so important to us? It's not just the indescribably addictive taste and texture. It's also down to a chemical produced in our brains called dopamine: essentially, we are all hard-wired to get hooked.

Before you even taste the chocolate, dopamine floods you with love, passion and desire, as you anticipate how delicious it's going to be and how it's going to make you feel. When you actually taste the chocolate, it has the same impact as any class-A drug hitting your brain. It's the aroma, the unique and unmistakable scent that overpowers you from your nose to your toes. It's sweet, sexual, rich and evocative – and we can never be satisfied with just one taste.

Chocolate is addictive and deeply sensory, but it's also part of our culture. It's ingrained in so many different societies; towns and communities have been built on it; it has fed soldiers at war and allowed us to enjoy some of the most innovative sweet products we will experience in our lifetimes. It's also at the root of a fierce competition between rival multinational chocolate companies as they battle it out to invent new and exciting ways to give us our daily hit of dopamine – and, of course, that sugar rush too.

My professional journey with chocolate began in 2004. However, looking back, chocolate was a huge part of my childhood, as it is for many of us. Most of my family festivities involved chocolate in one way or another: Easter, Christmas, birthdays, anniversaries and even casual get-togethers always included chocolate biscuits, cakes or bars. This was the start of my love affair with chocolate. My passion for anything sweet was with me from birth, thanks to all the women around me who could bake. Baking was a part of all our lives, particularly on Sundays. Every Sunday, arriving promptly at midday, my family would all meet for lunch at my grandma's house – but it was after lunch when the kitchen really came to life. Tea time was at 5pm, with more extended family arriving to sit around the dining table, which would be heaving with cakes, scones, corned beef pie, apple pie, jelly, chocolate crispy cakes, fairy buns and lots more. There was always a lot to prepare, and we didn't have long to get everything ready: very much like my days as a pastry chef, when everything had to be ready for the start of service. As soon as I was able, I was there alongside my mum and grandma making cakes and learning how to juggle everything so it was all ready at 5pm on the dot. Most Sundays, the spread included a chocolate cake with an entire big bar of Cadbury Dairy Milk melted and smothered over the top.

During the week, we rarely had sweets and chocolate, but on Sundays, if we had been on our best behaviour, my brother and I were allowed to pick two – yes, *two* – chocolate bars from the sweet tub in the pantry. There was always a variety to choose from, and my grandma made sure to always have two of each type so my brother and I wouldn't fight over the same bar. I'm talking mainstream confectionery bars, like Aero®, Drifter, Twix, Cadbury Dairy Milk and Texan. We definitely got our sugar hit every week.

A school trip to Paris in 1987 changed so much for me: drinking hot chocolate and eating a croissant in the Moulin Rouge Café for breakfast was mesmerising to me. The hot chocolate was intensely chocolatey, and it came in a bowl, not a mug, that seemed to be the size of a mixing bowl, while the freshly baked croissant had paper-light layers of pastry and a buttery aftertaste. This was the moment I experienced a new style of baking, and I mentally noted all the patisseries we passed on that trip: I thought they looked incredible compared to the bakeries back home. There is beauty in both, of course, but I was captivated by the refined look of French pastries.

I decided to train as a chef and continued to pursue my love of patisserie. College took me back to Paris in 1991 for a professional expo. I was a bit older, with some skills under my belt and some knowledge of French patisserie and its incredible attention to detail. There were techniques I was eager to learn, and flavours and textures I was impatient to experience. I had just discovered an interest in fashion the same year, and going to Paris meant I could experiment with fashion as much as I wanted. I knew that I wanted to make an impression: to express that I was creative and refined. OK, and I wanted to just feel *free*; to be flamboyant and express myself like Madonna had with her 1990 *Blond Ambition* tour. I was inspired by her and fed my creativity through music as well as food.

Now that I was training to be a chef, I looked at the Parisian patisserie in a very different way, and noticed that, sitting alongside many of the famous patissier's pastries, there were fine chocolates. They were mainly dark chocolate, and looked so precise and neat, worlds away from the sweet and buttery Belgian and British chocolates I had previously experienced. They were incredibly luxurious, handmade and intense in both their aroma and taste. They made an instant and lasting impact on me. For years after, I continued to visit Paris, exploring and looking for new chocolatiers and patissiers, but not yet knowing that one day, I too would become a world-renowned chocolatier.

The years up to and including the start of my business in 2006 were an important part of my journey. I had to try as many different types of chocolate as I could, and I can vividly recall the joy and happiness I experienced as I visited chocolate shops, chocolate festivals and cacao plantations, discovering the world of chocolate – and, of course, the people who make it all happen.

This book is a celebration and appreciation of all things chocolate: not just the cacao beans, but the growers, the chocolate producers, the chocolatiers, the marketing and branding teams – and you. Without you, we would not be celebrating this wonderful, unique food. I'm sharing this book with you to show you that chocolate is not just brown (which is the least glamorous colour on the planet). As you hold my book in your hands, I hope you will be dazzled by its colours and design. I want you to feel what I feel when surrounded by all this joy. Forget brown: praise the cacao pod, which is vibrant and colourful when ripe; celebrate the dazzling branding and packaging of chocolate, with colours so bold and vibrant they scream at you from the shelves; and most of all, discover the colourful and creative people behind everything in the chocolate world.

You will need:

- airtight containers
- artist's paintbrushes
- baking parchment
- balloon whisk
- chocolate scraper or wallpaper scraper
- cotton and vinyl food-handling gloves
- deco transfer sheets
- digital thermometer
- dipping forks
- edible shimmer powders
- electric heat gun (paint-stripper)
- fat-soluble chocolate colouring
- food processor
- granite or stone pestle and mortar
- hairdryer
- immersion blender
- metal mixing bowls
- notepad and pencil
- palette knife
- piping bag and nozzles (including doughnut filling nozzle)
- sharp knife
- silicone spatula
- timer

The cacao pod, cacao beans and chocolate

I promised you a colourful journey, and the colour starts here. If you have never seen cacao pods ripening on the tree, then brace yourself for an explosion of colour. Most of us have a fascination with chocolate in its finished form, be that a bar, a bonbon, a drink or a cake. However, I am yet to meet anyone who doesn't find themselves captivated and mesmerised by the look, feel and colours of the cacao pod when they first see, hold and taste the seed inside.

My first cacao pod

My memory of holding my first cacao pod (or *Theobroma cacao*, which translates as 'the food of the gods') is as vivid as any significant life event. I travelled to Guayaquil in Ecuador in 2008 to take part in ChocoFest, a festival and celebration of all things Ecuadorian chocolate and cacao. I travelled with my good friend James, who was there to photograph the trip and experience the Ecuadorian hospitality and chocolate with me. To say we were welcomed with open arms is very much an understatement: our hosts were wholeheartedly joyous and vibrant. Their enthusiasm was so surprising to me. Don't get me wrong, I'm not a miserable person – far from it! – but it did highlight how reserved we can be in the UK when it comes to how we express our joy. Cacao is vibrant and colourful, and everyone around us was, too.

As part of this amazing trip we were going to visit a cacao plantation. This would be my first experience of seeing cacao trees growing – and, in fact, the first time I had seen a cacao bean in its pure wet form, straight out of the pod.

The drive to the plantation was like any other drive, until we reached a simple turning point where the tarmac changed in an instant to a dirt road with dramatic potholes. The surrounding scenery was lush and striking. I guess my naivety showed as we drove deeper into the rainforest until we were miles from any town or the concrete buildings of the city. I remember being thrown around the jeep and holding on tightly as we drove along the riverside, passing banana and mango trees, neither of which I had

Cacao pods growing in the village of Kumily in Kerala, India. Cacao pods come in a range of vibrant colours, including green, red, orange and purple.

ever seen growing in the wild before. Seeing these tropical fruits growing in abundance on the trees mesmerised me; it still does, to this day.

Another moment of that drive I will never forget was seeing cattle enjoying the cooling waters of a fast-moving, murky-looking river, while locals washed their clothes on rocks at the river's edge. I had only seen images like these on TV, and I took a few seconds to reflect on all we had at home: a plumbed-in washing machine, running water and, well, every kind of appliance possible. We had some amazing people guiding us and giving us all the information about the area and the local people. There was no running water; some people had wired electricity or a generator, and so had some form of lighting when the sun set. It was basic and beautiful, and it could be a real shock to see, every few miles, a fridge stacked with bottled water. We were told that bottled water was more expensive than petrol, which blew my mind.

THE CACAO POD, CACAO BEANS AND CHOCOLATE

Finally, we approached the point where we would need to get out of the jeep and walk the rest of the way to the cacao plantation. It was incredibly humid and hot, so armed with sturdy shoes, sun cream, lots of insect repellent and my sun hat, we set off. We were guided through a tiny village made up of just a few houses that had been made using anything available. Everyone had a chicken or two, a dog or two, and a huge smile for us when we said hello.

Something I had not anticipated is that cacao trees are not grown in open fields or on flat ground. Instead, there were huge mango trees, towering over banana trees, which in turn towered over the cacao trees. In the dappled sunlight, the cacao trees looked as if they had been randomly scattered across the uneven landscape, although I'm sure they were all strategically planted with all the precision needed for many successful harvests. There was so much to take in that I'm sure I missed much of the information the cacao farmer was sharing with us. I didn't even spot the cacao pods on the trees until, with great excitement, some other members of our group pointed out ripe pods hanging on the trees. There they were: the birthplace of chocolate. They weren't brown, nor did they resemble chocolate in any way. They were unlike any fruit I had ever seen.

The pods could be described as alien: they looked like something from another world, with their unusually knobbly and textured tough outer rind. Some were tiny, the size of your thumbnail, then others on the same tree were the size of an egg, or even of a small rugby ball. The smaller pods were green and not ripe; however, the larger pods' colours had vibrant yellows and reds with bold green splashes and speckles. They were so shiny, it was like they were crying out to be picked before they burst open with ripeness.

The farmer was wielding a machete-style knife that was hooked at the end so the pods could be easily plucked from the tree. He held

Cacao growing countries

Africa: Liberia, Sierra Leone, Ghana, Ivory Coast, Nigeria, Togo, Equatorial Guinea, Congo, Sao Tome, Cameroon, Gabon, Democratic Republic of Congo, Madagascar, Uganda, Tanzania

Asia: Malaysia, The Philippines, India, China (Yunnan Province), Cambodia, Thailand, Vietnam, Myanmar, Indonesia, Sri Lanka

South Pacific: Australia, Papua New Guinea, Solomon Islands, Fiji, Samoa, Vanuatu, Timor-Leste

North and Central America: Costa Rica, USA (Hawaii, Puerto Rico), Mexico, Guatemala, Belize, El Salvador, Honduras, Panama, Nicaragua

Caribbean: Saint Vincent and the Grenadines, Dominican Republic, Haiti, Jamaica, Cuba, Dominica, Trinidad and Tobago, Grenada, Saint Lucia

South America: Brazil, Peru, Bolivia, Venezuela, Guyana, Colombia, Ecuador

a ripe pod in his hand, and, with the precision of a surgeon, cut into the pod, just deeply enough to avoid damaging any of the seeds inside – these are precious, so care is needed not to cut them. He pulled half of the pod away, revealing what I can only explain as the most unusual – and inedible – looking thing I have ever seen in my career as a chef and chocolatier. The seeds, or cacao beans, sat side by side in tightly packed rows that ran in straight lines from top to bottom of the pod. They were covered with a creamy white mucilage, making them slippery and a bit slimy. At this point, cameras were going off as rapidly as if Madonna had just left the building, and oohs and aahs were filling the forest air. I was struck by how the Ecuadorians, who had seen these before, some of them daily, still showed as much excitement for the beans as we did seeing them for the first time. We were encouraged to taste the beans, and told not to bite into them, but just to taste the outer coating. It was slippery and semi-sweet, a bit like a lychee, and not at all what I was expecting. Did I like it? Not really. The farmer then blew my mind by cutting open an individual bean and revealing something even more alien than the pod itself. The bean had a pinky-purple hue that blended into white; it looked like a tightly put together jigsaw of random segments. It was the most beautiful bean, seed, food, botanical thing I had ever seen, and more paparazzi-style photography took place. At this point, there was no resemblance to chocolate at all: nothing brown in colour or creamy in texture; no intoxicating roasting aromas, and nothing close to the chocolate I knew. Our visit to the plantation seemed so short and I know that many of us would have liked to stay longer, just to absorb the atmosphere and admire those beautiful trees, heaving with colourful pods and delicate, tiny flowers.

Cultivating cacao

There is a narrow strip around the Earth that has just the right conditions for growing cacao, which is why we don't see it growing in non-equatorial climates. Having said that, if you ever visit the Eden Project or Kew Gardens in the UK, and other botanical gardens around the world, you may see some cacao trees successfully growing and fruiting in hot houses. But that narrow strip, stretching roughly 10 degrees north and south of the equator, is where the magic really happens, and where we see whole plantations of cacao being cultivated. It's hot, rainy and humid: cacao trees love a rainforest, and need the right balance between sun but not too much sun, and a temperature of 18–30°C (64–86°F). Quite a specific environment – and a delicate one, too, which is why we need to protect it if we are to continue growing cacao beans to make chocolate for generations to come.

The cacao tree

It blows my mind when I think about how cacao happens to be – to just *be*. It's amazing to think that we have something so incredibly special, which has made its way into our lives over thousands of years. I do believe it really was a gift from the gods or the sky people. As a chocolatier, I constantly remind myself that the chocolate I use to create my products is the *actual bean*, from an ancient tree in an ancient land. It has been with us for such a long time.

Cacao trees are quite beautiful, standing 4.5–7.5m (15–25 feet) high, with long, leathery leaves that begin their lives red in colour then turn green as they mature. Keeping the trees well pruned and looked after is important. All harvesting of the pods is done by hand with a machete or a blade on a long pole; no machine can harvest cacao pods, so it's incredibly labour-intensive.

Here is something pretty special about the cacao tree and her pods. All cacao trees blossom from the branches and the trunk, then the cacao pods begin to develop if each flower has been pollinated by a fly. The tree can have ripe and ripening pods at the same time as having flowers ready to be pollinated: it's amazing. The flowers are tiny and have no scent, but they are stunning close up.

Those alien-looking pods start their life green, then transition through yellow, gold, red, burgundy: a whole mix of colours (there are even some browns in there too). They are so colourful and vibrant, it can really take your breath away. In fact, when I visited cacao grower Frank Homann's plantations and nursery in Honduras, I was blown away by a heritage variety he was cultivating called Mayan Red. The pods on the trees were a uniformly saturated rich red. They didn't look real; they could have been hand-painted sculptures of pods stuck on the branches and trunks of the trees. Not even Pantone could have created such a saturated, intense red.

After their colourful outside, the creamy white mucilage that covers every seed inside can look a bit dull, but still unusual. When you split open a cacao pod, you should try the seed/bean: it's acidic, fruity and mouth-watering. As the farmer told me on my first plantation trip, don't chew the seed to break through that fruity mucilage: you will hit intense bitterness, so bitter that you will spit it out. Inside, the seed is soft and a bit spongy, with varying hues of pure porcelain white, lilac, purple, beige and a touch of pink. I think they are quite stunning: natural works of art. If you look closely, you can see that they are made up of random segments, with a twisting germ ready to germinate and grow into a new tree.

If I had to choose one word to describe the wet cacao beans, it would be slimy. At this stage, the beans are packed into sacks in bulk to be taken for fermenting. Did you know cacao beans were fermented? I certainly didn't when I first started

Did you know?
A cacao tree can easily celebrate its 100th birthday, but it is likely to bear fruit for only half of its lifetime.

THE JOY OF CHOCOLATE

experimenting with chocolate. This essential part of the process of transforming bean to chocolate is not commonly known, and rarely mentioned in any advertising by larger chocolate companies.

So what does fermenting do? To put it simply, the process destroys the mucilage coating on the seed, kills the germ, and generates and develops flavours in the beans. It's a complex process that has to be carefully controlled, as it plays a vital role in what the final chocolate will taste like.

A beautiful cacao tree on a plantation in Brazil, abundant with ripe, colourful pods.

Cacao bean varieties

First of all, let's dispel the myth that there are only three varieties of cacao bean. Perhaps you haven't heard that myth before, but it's commonly claimed that there are only three varieties: Criollo, Trinitario and Forastero. In fact, there are at least ten known hybrid varieties of cacao, and the three that get the exposure may not be quite as they seem at first glance.

Criollo

When I first entered the chocolate industry in 2004, there was one variety everyone was talking about: Criollo. People said it was the queen of cacao beans, the very best variety, the rarest, and that its chocolate tasted pure, as close as possible to what the Aztecs would have tasted. It does make some absolutely stunning chocolate, but all taste is down to personal preference and how the chocolate has been made by the chocolate maker. Reputation plays a part in everything we taste: food fashions flood in and out, and there are a lot of very romantic and dramatic stories, myths and legends around cacao. Its history is as vibrant as the colour of the pods, and as complex as the flavours of the beans. I, and many other industry professionals, do not agree with Criollo being labelled the best variety. Criollo accounts for a very, very small amount of the cacao grown globally. Anything that isn't grown in abundance will feel rare in comparison to its more common cousins, which creates a sense of stir and excitement.

Spanish colonisers in Mexico and Central America named the first cacao they found Criollo, meaning 'native'. But was Criollo actually native to the area in which they found it? The answer is no – cacao originates in the Amazon rainforest. According to many studies into exactly where, it looks like cacao originally comes from the point where Colombia, Ecuador, Peru and Brazil meet.

Criollo pods are generally yellow and red, although some are green. The beans inside range from pale purple to pure white (the 'Porcelana' variety). If you have tasted chocolate made with Criollo beans, then you will know that it has a low bitterness, it's quite delicate and has a soft acidity. It's easy to eat as a dark chocolate, and I often experience berry jam notes and a creaminess that, in dark chocolate, is pretty wonderful. It's aromatic, but for me it lacks some of the complexities I enjoy with other varieties.

Trinitario

You could say that Trinitario is the most famous hybrid bean in the world. It was developed as the result of a devastating hurricane hitting Trinidad in 1727 and almost wiping out its Criollo plantations.

Forastero beans were brought from Venezuela and cross-fertilised with Criollo beans, giving us Trinitario. The pods of the Trinitario are less bumpy and lumpy than Criollo, and the beans are often smaller, ranging in colour from light to dark purple. Having two different beans as parents brings us some complex and super-gorgeous chocolate. I find the flavours of Trinitario nostalgic, deeply chocolatey and comforting. If you haven't tried it, then once you get to know it, you will love it.

Forastero

Back in my early days of being a chocolatier, the Forastero was described to me as 'the stranger in the room'. Why? Well, it literally translates as 'stranger'. This bean is predominantly cultivated in Brazil, South East Asia and West Africa, and its pods are smoother than the others, coloured with vibrant yellows and reds, and sometimes purples and oranges, which really shine. You will all have tasted chocolate made with Forastero beans, as this variety is often used in confectionery and mass-market chocolate. I need to say very clearly that this does not mean it's not a beautiful cacao bean. Forastero is *the* chocolatey taste we all love. It's the taste of your first-ever chocolate button, your first sip of hot chocolate; it's the memory of chocolate you will have for the rest of your life. However, in fine chocolate circles it can often be dismissed as less complex, and less interesting, even though it's the most prolific bean. It just doesn't have the fancy label. But the joy of chocolate includes that you can buy from your local supermarket, which is probably predominantly made from the Forestero bean or a blend of this and the Trinitario bean (although mainstream chocolate products rarely name the cacao bean used in their composition).

Nacional

I have to tell you about this bean variety, as I have fallen head over heels in love with it. If cacao beans were children and I had to pick a favourite, then this would be it. It's called Nacional or Pure Arriba Nacional. It's found in South America, and I first came across it in Ecuador in 2010 in chocolate bar form – no flavours, no inclusions and nowhere to hide flavours. Nacional offered a flavour and character I had never before experienced in any chocolate. It's quite a rare variety – in fact, it was believed by many to be extinct until it was rediscovered in the 21st century. All I can say is that you must try it. If you see a bar of Ecuadorian or Peruvian fine chocolate made with this bean variety, then grab it. It's unusually intoxicating: soft, delicate and complex all at the same time.

Did you know?
While the pulp from around the bean is not used in the production of chocolate, it can be made into a pretty potent alcoholic drink, or used to make sorbet and even jam.

The composition of chocolate

Chocolate has hundreds of chemical compounds that allow us to taste up to 800 flavours and tastes. Some of them can react with chemicals in our brains and alter how we feel. This is what makes tasting and eating chocolate and experiencing the different varieties so exciting and unique.

Theobromine

This chemical has a bitter taste and a similar molecular structure to caffeine, so can give you that familiar feeling of stimulation when consumed. Theobromine has also been found to dilate blood vessels and stimulate the heart and nerve endings. When I taste a lot of dark chocolate, I feel a tingling in my fingertips and on my head and I struggle to sleep. This was great for writing my book – a few squares of 80 per cent, and I could write for a few more hours!

Phenylethylamine

Again a bitter-tasting chemical, but a key factor in how chocolate makes us feel lighter, uplifted and happy.

Caffeine

Caffeine is present in cacao and chocolate, but in very small amounts. Some studies show it can help reduce inflammation. Again, it is a stimulant – as we all know when we drink tea and coffee.

Metals

Cacao also contains natural salts composed of naturally occurring metals, such as magnesium, potassium, calcium and iron. Many of the compounds found in chocolate have a bitter taste, which we associate with poison or something not to be eaten or enjoyed. Sugar balances this bitterness, allowing us – and our brains – to enjoy the hundreds of other taste and flavour compounds contributing to chocolate's complexity. Most chocolate that isn't 100 per cent cocoa solids will contain a sweetener of some kind, commonly cane sugar, beet sugar, coconut nectar sugar or artificial sweetener. These sugars are ground down, which increases their surface area, and then enrobed by cocoa butter during the conching process (see page 25). Using a non-sugar sweetener, such as sugar alcohols or stevia powder, changes the composition and mouthfeel of the chocolate, sometimes making it taste sweeter and at times giving a slightly bitter aftertaste. Erythritol is one sweetener that is becoming more commonly used. It has a cooling effect in the mouth, which changes how you experience a chocolate's flavour. This can detract from the complexities of dark chocolate, especially single-bean varieties, but as many governments advise us to limit our sugar consumption, these alternative sweeteners will be used more, and in time, we will become accustomed to the taste.

How do cacao beans become chocolate?

Harvesting

Ripe pods are picked and cut from the trees by hand using sharp blades, carried in baskets on the harvesters' backs and then put into sacks on the forest floor – from where their very long journey begins.

The pods are then split open to release the beans. This is done still on the plantation, and the action is performed by hand with a machete. I think your mind probably just went to the same place mine does every time I think about this. It's dangerous work, and, yes, the workers do sometimes get injured.

Fermentation

The wet cacao beans are then removed from the pods before being scooped into wooden boxes covered with jute sacks and/or banana leaves. When the beans are removed from the pods, they are sterile, but naturally occurring yeasts and bacteria from the environment, people's hands and the equipment will make their way on to the beans, and once they are trapped under the sacks and leaves, the fermentation process begins. The actual bean beneath the mucilage does not ferment: it's just the mucilage that does. The triggers for the fermentation process are yeasts, enzymes and bacteria, with the whole process taking six to ten days.

The next stage of fermentation is called the anaerobic phase. Anaerobic conditions are environments lacking oxygen. In cacao, the pulp surrounding the beans creates a wet shield that blocks air from entering the mass of beans in the fermentation boxes. The mucilage is made up of water, high levels of sugars (sucrose, glucose, fructose) and various different acids. The sugar and the acidity creates an ideal environment for microorganisms to work in. The three key components in the process are yeasts, lactic acid-producing bacteria

> **Did you know?**
> Whether or not drinking chocolate should be allowed during fasting periods was the cause of religious debate in the 17th century. Pope Alexander VII eventually settled the matter by decreeing that all liquids were allowed during fasts.

and pulp enzymes. Yeasts quickly consume simple sugars and produce carbon dioxide, ethanol and low amounts of energy. Meanwhile, lactic acid-producing bacteria convert the citric acid, glucose and other carbohydrates in the pulp into lactic acid. The production of ethanol and lactic acid is visible from the bubbles of carbon dioxide that will appear on the surface of the wet beans. During this process, the beans will also give off an aroma that is a mix of fizzy, astringent, cheesy and alcoholic. It's a really lovely smell, and one you will only experience on a cacao plantation where fermentation is happening.

The next stage is the aerobic phase, when the beans are mixed and moved to an empty fermentation box, therby introducing oxygen. This stage generates heat within the beans, along with acetic acid-producing bacteria. The process oxidises the ethanol and citric, malic and lactic acids. The acetic acid then breaks down further to carbon dioxide and water. Breaking down ethanol is a reaction that creates energy, which is where all that heat comes from. Turning the beans allows heat to escape, meaning the overall temperature will drop. However it will build back up again as more oxygen is introduced. This process may be repeated in further fresh fermentation boxes. The intense heat combined with the release of ethanol and acetic acid within the cacao beans breaks down

Cacao pods being harvested by hand in Ekoumdoum, Cameroon – the only way to harvest cacao.

THE JOY OF CHOCOLATE

the cell walls of the beans. This means that they are no longer able to germinate, and their internal structure becomes a hive of chemical activities that develop the flavour precursors that give chocolate its distinctively chocolatey taste.

The beans are then spread out on raised mesh beds (or, in some areas, on the ground) to dry in the hot equatorial sun. They must be turned often, and can't be allowed to get wet from the forest rain, as this would cause them to mould and spoil. At this stage, the beans become a dry brown colour and develop a hard shell or skin. Drying the beans reduces their moisture content from 60 per cent to 8 per cent or below. Drying must be controlled and done well so that the beans do not mould or rot when they are packed up and shipped across the world.

Transport

What a journey so far. And there is still a huge way to travel – quite literally – before we have what we know as a chocolate bar or bonbon in our hands. In chapter three, I will explore micro-batch or craft chocolate, and we'll learn about creating chocolate in a more artisanal way, but first, let's talk about how cacao beans get from the plantation to the factory to create our best-known and most-loved chocolate bars. The journey begins where the beans were dried on the plantation: once dried, they are put into jute sacks. These are breathable, which is very important, as the cacao beans need to be able to breathe in order to prevent mould or rot. What happens next depends on where in the world you are, as each country, government or controlling body and plantation is different.

Some plantations are very close to the facilities for processing the beans into chocolate. Casa Luker, for example, is a family-owned and -run Colombian chocolate company that has been operating since 1906. They grow their own beans and then process them into chocolate, so the beans don't have to travel far to be processed. But this isn't the norm. Most of the cacao in the world travels vast distances around the globe to reach the factories where it will be processed into chocolate. The beans get to producers in a number of different ways, so to explain in detail I am quoting the International Cocoa Organisation (ICCO), an intergovernmental organisation established in 1973 under the auspices of the United Nations and operating within the framework of successive International Cocoa Agreements.

The ICCO explains:

When discussing cocoa trading, a clear distinction has to be made between the actual or physical markets and the futures or terminal markets. Nearly all cocoa coming from origin countries is sold through the physical market. The physical market involves the type of business that most people normally think of when talking about trading in commodities. The structure and length of the cocoa marketing channels differ from region to region within the same producing country as well as across producing countries. At one extreme of the spectrum, the marketing channel between cocoa farmers and exporters encompasses at least two middlemen: small traders and wholesalers. Small traders buy cacao beans directly from farmers, visiting them one by one. In a second stage, small buyers sell the beans to wholesalers, who in turn will resell them to exporters. At the other extreme of the spectrum, cacao beans are sold directly to exporters by farmers' cooperatives or even directly exported by the co-operative.

Once cacao beans reach the port of export, they are stocked in warehouses, while being graded and subsequently loaded on to cargo vessels. Warehouses should have cement and non-flammable floors without cracks and crevices where insects can hide. Ideally, the floor level of the warehouse should be higher than the surrounding land to prevent flooding and to allow water to flow away. In some producing countries, cacao beans are processed in the conditioning plants, most of them located in port warehouses because of the high moisture level of the beans and a high variance in their quality. Conditioning — either by hand or mechanically — is also used to blend poor-quality with good-quality beans.

Once cacao beans have been graded and loaded into cargo vessels, they are shipped either in new jute bags or in bulk. In recent years, shipment of cacao beans in bulk has been growing in popularity because it can be up to one third cheaper than conventional shipment in jute bags. Loose cacao beans are loaded either in shipping containers or directly into the hold of the ship, the so-called 'mega-bulk' method. The latter mode is often adopted by larger cocoa processors.

Transforming beans into chocolate

Now it's time to start transforming the fermented, dried cacao beans into chocolate. One of my most-loved chocolate brands is Guittard Chocolate from San Francisco, a family-owned company with a 150-year history of making chocolate from the bean. Their journey started in 1868, when Etienne Guittard travelled from Tournus, France, to San Francisco with the aim of making his fortune in the California Gold Rush. He brought chocolate from his uncle's factory to trade, and realised that wealthy miners were prepared to pay well for his chocolate treats. Travelling back to France, he refined his skills in chocolate making before returning to San Francisco in 1868, where he opened a store on Sansome Street selling chocolate, tea, coffee and spices. I bet his shop had the most wonderful smell and looked stunning, with shelves filled to the ceiling. The Guittard family is still making chocolate today, and I'm really honoured to call them all friends. It's important to get all the details accurate, so I had the joy of speaking to Gary Guittard, President and CEO of Guittard, to ask how his company makes chocolate from the bean.

Arrival at the factory

Gary is passionate about working directly with the cacao growers, working with them from the very beginning and through the important stage of fermentation, as Guittard's various chocolate recipes demand different fermentation times. Once the beans are received at the factory, they are thoroughly cleaned – it's very important that nothing gets into the chocolate-making process that is not a cacao bean. There are bacteria and pathogens on the beans that arrive at Guittard, so the goods in that area are kept separate from the rest of the factory so that there is no cross-contamination at any stage (the bacteria/pathogens are destroyed/killed off during the roasting process that follows). All the beans need to be cleared in the lab for flavour and to check that what was ordered is what has actually arrived.

A beautiful Guittard Chocolate advertising poster from 1872. The advert features their factory in San Francisco, and scenes of the chocolate–making process.

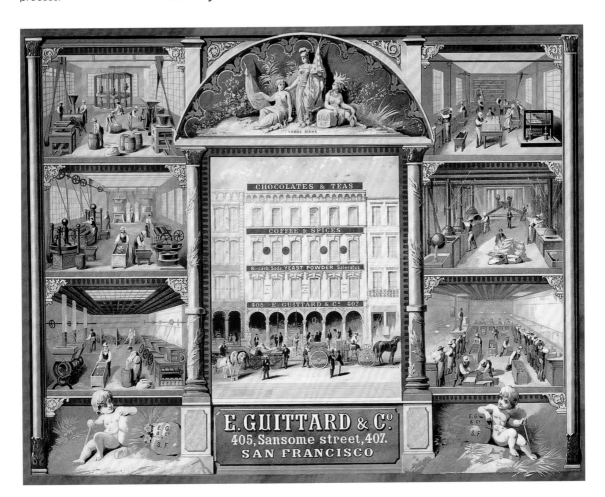

Roasting

Now for the roasting process. Guittard has many different roasting times for each bean variety to celebrate all the diversities of flavour that can be developed and nurtured. You can't roast all the different beans at the same temperature in the same way. The type of bean dictates how it should be roasted. Every chocolate maker has their own time and temperature of roast so this is a guideline I have used. Preheat a fan assisted oven and the temperature can vary from 120 to 160°C (250 to 325°F). Beans are laid flat onto trays and roasted for any time between 10 and 25 minutes. The beans are allowed to cool before they can be winnowed to separate the bean from the husk. Mass market chocolate bean roasting happens in digitally controlled rotating hot air ovens so the beans get a very even roasting time.

Winnowing

Once the beans have been roasted, it's time for the winnowing process. This is where hammers crack open the beans, and the broken beans – now called 'nibs' – flow through sieves or screens of different sizes. The loose shells get blown off, so only the nibs are left.

Grinding

There are different grinding protocols for the nibs, depending on the bean varieties. Grinding releases the cocoa butter from the bean, creating a grainy liquid. This is now chocolate liquor, which can be used as an unsweetened baking chocolate. It is then passed through rollers to reduce the particle size to make it smooth. This happens in stages. The delicate flavours need to be maintained, so it's a careful process for each variety. The liquor can be pressed to create cocoa powder and butter, or refined to make chocolate.

Pressing

Gary explains that, in the old days, adding sugar to the chocolate liquor was not possible, as it would not hold together. So the only option was drinking chocolate – until van Houten invented the cacao press, which can be used to create both cocoa butter and cocoa powder.

The chocolate liquor is pressed to release the cocoa butter, which is added into chocolate during refining and conching to coat all the sugar, helping it hold together so it sets as a bar of chocolate. The 'cake' that's left over is ground up to create cocoa powder.

Refining

If you want to make dark chocolate, you take the chocolate liquor created by grinding and add sugar and cocoa butter. Once this has been mixed together, it needs to go through a two-roller refiner, which runs at two different speeds. Because one roller moves faster than the other, it shears the particles, which reduces the particle size until you have a very thick paste with a texture a bit like soft clay. Because the sugar particles have been reduced in size, increasing their surface area, there is now not enough fat to coat all the sugar. The mixture weaves its way through five further refining rollers, with each roller moving a bit faster than the one below it. As it travels through the five rollers, the paste shears more and more, reducing the particle size still further until it comes out of the refiner looking like a flaky powder.

Conching

The refined chocolate liquor is then transferred into a conche to be mixed. This is a key area of chocolate making, so it's vital that it is carefully carried out. The conche is like a cooking vessel that mixes the chocolate back and forth in a non-stop process, creating the maillard reaction, which develops toasty flavours by cooking the carbohydrates in the chocolate. The conche will run for 12–72 hours without stopping, and the temperature can reach 93°C (200°F). More cocoa butter is added at the later stages of the conching process, along with cacao liquor, depending on the recipe of the chocolate that's being made. It is then removed from the conche, and the viscosity is adjusted depending on the recipe specification so that the chocolate can be used for different applications.

Tempering and finishing

Finally, it's run through the tempering machine and made into bars, chocolate chips or chocolate wafers (buttons) to be packaged and sent to chefs and chocolatiers like myself all over the world.

So, there you go: it's an epic journey from bean to bar, and requires a very technical process to ensure the same quality and taste every time. Ultimately, though, you cannot make a poor-quality cacao bean taste amazing, so we have the growers to thank for cultivating with care and fermenting with precision.

Did you know?
The Ivory Coast is the world's largest exporter of cacao beans, responsible for over 40% of global production.

Some useful terminology

Origin

'Single origin' is a term that has become a beacon for high quality, but I'm here to tell you that single origin does not guarantee you a fantastic bar of chocolate. Single origin means that the beans used in the chocolate are from one country or one region – and that's it. It's not promising you anything else. I've had the joy of trying some of the world's finest single origins, and some have blown me away, like Bare Bones of Glasgow Dominican Republic dark chocolate, which is so intoxicating and wonderful that it's up there as one of my all-time favourite dark chocolates. On the other hand, I've had single-origin chocolate that had very little sparkle and tasted dull, dull, dull. So don't automatically assume single-origin chocolate will be the very best chocolate. It can, however, be a fantastic advertisement for the country of origin.

Blended chocolate

I'm a huge fan of blended chocolate varieties. There are two ways to look at blends: we can have a single-origin blended chocolate, or a blended chocolate with multiple origins. A blended chocolate will have beans of different varieties, which makes it really interesting as the different varieties all add something to the flavour. When looking at the flavour profile of blended chocolate, it can be quite a roller coaster of a flavour journey, with peaks and troughs that should be well balanced and complement each other.

Single-bean

Single-bean chocolate can be very special, but, just like single origin, it doesn't automatically mean it's going to be a spectacular chocolate. 'Single bean' means just that: only one bean variety has been used to make the chocolate, so all the character of that bean is celebrated in the end result. I find single-bean chocolate fascinating, as it's so pure and simple in its construction. Again, however, I have had both fantastic and average single-bean chocolate. One of the standout single-bean chocolate bars I have enjoyed is Land Chocolate 73% Nicaragua, which is made with the Nicaliso cacao bean. It's an excellent example of using a vibrant bean, and has characters of black olives, grapefruit and orange.

Did you know?
When English pirates seized a Spanish ship containing cacao beans in the 16th century, they thought the beans were sheep droppings and destroyed them.

Single-plantation

Single-plantation chocolate can be made from a single bean or a blend of beans, as long as the beans are from just one plantation, in one place. Chocolate maker Bertil Akesson owns his own cacao plantations and makes chocolate from his beans. A star of his collection is his Brazil 75%, from his plantation Fazenda Sempre Firme in Bahia. It is intensely dark and robust, with a very well-rounded finish.

I don't want to confuse you, but you can have chocolate that is single-origin, single-plantation and single-bean all at the same time (or just single-origin and single-plantation, but not single-bean). It makes choosing your fine chocolate an exciting journey. Most mainstream dark chocolate bars available in our supermarkets are blended and do not show their origin or bean varieties. This doesn't mean they are inferior, but they will not be as complex or have the same nuances fine chocolate bars have.

Types of chocolate

Dark chocolate

I will say this only once, so that I'm very clear: *dark chocolate should never and can never be called plain chocolate.* There is nothing plain about it; it's quite the opposite. Simply put, it is the purest way to experience the cacao bean in all its fantastic and characterful glory, made with just cacao beans and cane sugar, and sometimes some added cocoa butter. There may occasionally be vanilla beans or extract added, or sometimes soy lecithin or sunflower lecithin to act as an emulsifier. Dark chocolate is naturally vegan and dairy-free (although you should always read the label). When it comes to cocoa percentages, though, remember that the percentage does not give you any indication of flavour, taste and quality.

If you are reading this and shouting, 'I don't like dark chocolate!' then I say back, you just haven't found the right one for you. Not all dark chocolate is strong and bitter. In fact, it shouldn't taste only bitter – and it should never taste burned. There are delicate, creamy and smooth dark chocolates available in the lower percentages (60–66 per cent cocoa solids) that are as sweet and smooth as a milk chocolate. One thing is guaranteed: the flavour and complexities will blow you away. So, next time you decide to buy dark chocolate, try something new: try out a single-origin chocolate, or sample a blend or a single-bean variety.

There are some things to remember: for it to count as fine chocolate (or just real chocolate), the only fat in your chocolate bar should be cocoa butter; there shouldn't be any vegetable oil or palm oil. Vanillin is a no-go. And if any milk has been added, it's not pure dark chocolate. Dark chocolate is the way chocolate producers celebrate everything the cacao bean holds within it. All the magical flavours and complexities are hidden within the bean, just waiting to escape, and every different origin, blend and bean variety will make dramatically different chocolate.

White chocolate

Is it really chocolate? I'm going to allow myself a brief rant about this subject, as I've been having the same conversations about it for nearly twenty years. So: Yes it is, yes it is, yes it *is* real chocolate. There, I've said it!

White chocolate is the natural fat from the cacao bean (cocoa butter) blended with sugar, milk powder, usually vanilla and sometimes a natural emulsifier, like sunflower oil or soy lecithin. So it contains absolutely no cacao mass or solids (the brown part of the cacao bean). I'm renaming white chocolate zero per cent chocolate. But it *is* chocolate – as long as, and only if, the only fat used in the chocolate is cocoa butter, as this comes from the cacao bean. I know I may be in the minority here, but to me it's just as special, important and interesting as chocolate that contains cocoa solids – and it can taste just as exciting, too, if it's made with non-deodorised cocoa butter. There are two types of cocoa butter, and the one you use dramatically changes the taste and experience. White chocolate made with deodorised cocoa butter will mainly taste of vanilla, with a rich, milky finish but absolutely no cacao bean flavour. On the other hand, if white chocolate is made with non-deodorised cocoa butter (sometimes called 'natural cocoa butter') then the flavour from the beans shines through.

Deodorised cocoa butter	Non–deodorised cocoa butter
Has no flavour or aroma	Has the intoxicating flavours and aromas of the cacao bean
Has a light, pale yellow colour	Has a rich yellow colour
Has had all the nutrients and colour stripped out	Is rich in vitamins and beneficial minerals
Is used to increase the fluidity of chocolate	Is great for white chocolate when you want the flavour of the cacao bean in the chocolate
Is commonly used in cosmetics and by beauty companies for its nourishing and moisturising effects	

Milk chocolate

Oh, I do love milk chocolate. I love it so very much: it's comfort, it's soul food, it's rewarding, and it's my happy place. I like milk chocolates of all varieties and qualities, meaning I get as much joy from a confectionery bar as I do from a single-origin fine milk chocolate. So many of you love it, too, and for many of us it's associated with childhood memories and nostalgia. We all have our favourite go-to milk chocolate bars.

So what is it that makes it milk chocolate? The process is the same as that for making dark chocolate, but with the addition of milk powder during the conching stage, those creamy flavours and mellow aftertastes are developed. Adding milk to cocoa is like adding it to tea or coffee: it smooths out the tannins and bitterness, mellows the flavour and adds some sweetness. Not all milk chocolate is the same, of course, and it's all down to the ingredients – especially the kind of milk used. Whole milk powder will deliver the creamiest milk chocolate, whereas whey powder or semi-skimmed milk powder will deliver a less luxurious and milky milk chocolate.

Milk chocolate doesn't always get the media coverage that single-origin dark chocolate enjoys, but there are single-origin milk chocolates, as well as blended bars that are just as complex and of the same high quality (and made from the same cacao beans). So give milk chocolate a chance next time, instead of automatically reaching for dark. Higher-percentage milk chocolate has become increasingly popular, and I love it. If you haven't tried it, it offers the perfect balance between smooth, creamy and milky, and intense, robust and complex. Mainstream confectionery milk chocolate is, of course, a totally different type of chocolate, and often contains added vegetable fats and flavourings. I am not a chocolate snob, though, and I can appreciate the flavour, texture and decades of expertise that have brought us some of the world's most famous chocolate brands, even though some are considered not to be true chocolate at all due to the very low percentage of cacao, high amounts of sugar and often artificial flavourings.

Vegan milk or mylk chocolate

Thanks to innovation in alternative milks, milk chocolate has progressed so much that we now have some amazing ways to enjoy it without the dairy. OK, it's not exactly the same as milk, so you have to be ready for a change in taste and sometimes texture, but it's pretty good. The most popular milk alternatives in chocolate making are rice milk, oat milk, coconut milk, soy milk and almond milk powders. It's still pretty early days for these dairy alternatives, and the only way to know what you like is to try them all. (Hooray!) So far, from my research in tasting as many kinds as possible, my preference is for either a nut milk or oat milk as the alternative. At the time of writing, I've just been introduced to Amatika, an almond-milk chocolate made by Valrhona. It's wonderfully creamy and smooth, and the closest vegan alternative to milk chocolate I've tasted. With 46 per cent cocoa solids and made with a single-origin Madagascan bean, it's a great balance of creamy with a touch of acidity. Remember, most dark chocolate is naturally vegan, as it should not contain any dairy or animal ingredients, so if you need to feed your craving and cannot find a vegan milk chocolate, then head to the dark chocolate aisle.

Blond chocolate

If you have never experienced blond chocolate, then this is something for you to hunt out: it's pure indulgence and very sweet. Blond chocolate is made by cooking white chocolate slowly until it caramelises and turns golden in colour and develops a toffee-like flavour. It's sort of halfway between white and milk chocolate, and as well as its caramel character, it sometimes has a biscuity aftertaste. It makes wonderful blondies and mousses, as it has a super silky-smooth texture.

If you have ever eaten Caramac®, which I recall from my childhood as being a caramel-toffee, super-sweet chocolate bar, then blond chocolate is similar in character. At the time of writing, Cadbury have recently launched Caramilk into the UK market, and it's really delicious (if you're reading this in Australia or New Zealand, you will already know exactly how delicious it is, as it's been available to you for quite some time). The Caramilk bar's only fat is cocoa butter (it contains no palm oils or vegetable fats). Great work, Cadbury – wouldn't it be great if *all* chocolate vegetable-fat free? I'm sure it would increase sales.

Another mainstream brand that I had the joy of working with at the beginning of my chocolate career is Magnum. Their Double Gold Caramel Billionaire ice-cream bar is dipped in blond chocolate and is a total joy to eat (although I suggest grabbing a box of three, as they're addictive and just one won't be enough).

Ruby chocolate

This is the most Instagrammable chocolate there is thanks to its striking colour (which is actually a vibrant pink rather than the ruby red the name suggests). In 2017, Belgian chocolate producer Barry Callebaut launched their ruby chocolate at a trade show in Shanghai. The build-up was huge, and it took the industry by storm. So, what is it?

Ruby chocolate is made with particular cacao beans that give a pink hue to the finished chocolate. It's not white chocolate with pink colouring – it contains around 40 per cent cocoa solids – and its flavour is a mix of sweet berries, delicate cacao and a touch of soft acidity. Ruby chocolate is now being used in mainstream chocolate bars, such as KitKats®, as well as by independent chocolatiers for impactful and colourful bonbons, cakes and cookies. It might not be the most intensely characterful and complex of chocolate, but it's fun and bright, and has definitely captured imaginations at this moment in time. I'm so interested to see how it lasts, how it develops and how it will be used within the industry.

Ruby chocolate — more pink than ruby in colour — has a fruity and delicate flavour.

Alternative-sugar chocolate

We cannot ignore the fact that we are all being encouraged to reduce the amount of sugar we consume on a daily basis, and all chocolate contains sugar (unless it's made with 100 per cent cocoa solids, and most of us wouldn't choose that as our go-to, day-to-day chocolate). Chocolate makers are now getting really innovative, and alternative sugars are becoming very popular. Guittard have tapped into the popularity of paleo and keto lifestyles with a coconut sugar dark chocolate, as well as two dark chocolates sweetened with stevia and erythritol (see page 194). They taste wonderful – very chocolatey, with a well-rounded aftertaste – and they perform like all other chocolate.

Chocolates made using coconut sugar have a toffee-like flavour with a rich and intense finish. Coconut sugar has a slightly lower glycaemic index than white sugar, so creates less of a spike in your blood when consumed. It also contains healthy fats that are known to lower cholesterol and heart disease. There are many other brands now making alternative-sugar chocolate, and they're definitely not a compromise in any way, so if you are looking for sugar alternatives, then hunt these out.

Confectionery chocolate

I've said it before, and I'll say it again: I am not a chocolate snob. And this means I can appreciate all kinds of chocolate, and take a real joy in the nostalgia that long-standing chocolate brands bring us. That's why I am including confectionery chocolate as a type of chocolate. After all, the chocolate we all see every day in the corner shop and supermarket is chocolate, right? It's a good question, actually. This is what I understand the difference to be between confectionery chocolate and 'real' chocolate: real chocolate has just one fat, cocoa butter, whereas most confectionery has additional fats, usually palm oil, mango kernel oil and other vegetable fats, which cheapen the product. Also, the cocoa percentage is usually frighteningly low in both milk and dark chocolate, which again makes the product cheaper to manufacture. This doesn't mean it's bad-tasting chocolate, it just means it's a different *kind* of chocolate. It's not going to have the complex nuances and cacao-bean characters of fine chocolate, and nor will there be the same kind of beneficial properties that higher-percentage chocolate carries with it. However, confectionery chocolate does make us smile, and evokes childhood memories when we enjoyed it as a reward or a special treat.

When it comes down to it, the only thing that really matters are these three questions: Do I love this chocolate? Do I want another piece? Would I buy it again? If you answer 'yes' to all of them, then it's time for a huge HOORAY!, as you have fallen in love.

Whichever chocolate you choose to enjoy, choose it with passion, enjoy it with love and be curious to try different types. Your journey is just beginning, and with the unbelievable choice available to us all, you won't have to eat the same chocolate bar twice (unless you want to!). Just take the time to choose your chocolate carefully, considering the occasion. A special craft chocolate bar is a perfect gift, after-dinner chocolate or a moment of calm for yourself, while a well-known confectionery bar can offer a nostalgic treat or a piece of soul food to give you an inner hug of joy.

Raw chocolate

Does raw chocolate really exist? Well, this debate has been active for some time and will continue to be, due to the word 'raw' being used incorrectly. I hear the term used a lot within the health-food sector, and often see products advertised with claims that their chocolate has been made with raw cacao. For food to be classed as 'raw', any cooking or heating cannot exceed 47°C (116°F), and temperatures reached during the fermentation process can exceed 50°C (122°F). In addition, unroasted cacao beans can carry harmful bacteria, such as *E. coli*, *Staphylococcus* and *Salmonella*, so ingesting anything made with unroasted beans could be very harmful. You should never make chocolate from unroasted beans that have not been treated.

I think the term 'raw' is inappropriate and incorrect in this context. It would be better to call it 'low-temperature roasted chocolate', because even some of the world's finest raw chocolate has been heat-treated in some way. One brand that stands out for me is Pacari, the most ethical chocolate producer in Ecuador. Their biodynamic chocolate has phenomenal complexities and is, quite simply, a divine dark chocolate. To say that Pacari cares about cacao is an understatement; their passion is off the scale when it comes to every tiny detail. I have been very privileged to know Pacari founder and owner Santiago Peralta since I began my own chocolate journey, and his enthusiasm for cacao, chocolate and a summer scarf – very dapper – is intoxicating. His hard work with an incredible team of growers has resulted in a huge wave of awards, respect and recognition within the industry. Pacari doesn't only make raw chocolate, but one of theirs was the first I tasted that floored me with its quality, complexity and purity. It's a wonderfully accomplished bar of chocolate. Pacari control the temperature the cacao beans reach during roasting so that they do not rise above 42°C (108°F). This means the complexities of the chocolate, as well as the high levels of antioxidants, are retained.

It's down to personal taste, of course, but generally I enjoy chocolate made with roasted beans more than I do low-temperature roasted, because roasting develops flavours and complexity. As I will say time and again, the only way to know is to taste.

Did you know?
The Aztec emperor Montezuma reportedly drank 50 cups of chocolate each day.

Eating chocolate and the etiquette of tasting

Do you eat your chocolate a little too quickly because it's just so delicious, enjoying its sweet intensity and creamy texture, feeling the joy from the tip of your tongue right down into your stomach? I do – with milk chocolate, at least. When it comes to dark chocolate, I'm more of a slow-motion eater, as it's so much more intense and complex. As much as I love dark chocolate, I have a soft spot for milk chocolate – I think lots of us do. It's very easy to eat due to its mellow taste, plus it's usually super-sweet and creamy, which we are all hard-wired to enjoy. It's also nostalgic and comforting: many of us have very strong memories of milk chocolate being a treat when we were young children, and those feelings stay with us into adulthood. The way we eat chocolate and the rituals around how we enjoy it develop as we taste and eat more throughout our lives, and it's something I find truly fascinating.

Think back to a time when you first enjoyed chocolate. It's unlikely you'll be able to remember your first-ever taste of chocolate, as it was probably when you were so young that your brain cannot find the memory. Instead, perhaps you will think about the first time you had a whole bar of chocolate to yourself, with no need for sharing; the first time you realised how wonderful it tasted, and that you wanted and needed more; the moment when you realised your life was going to need to have chocolate in it on a very regular basis. Take the time to examine that memory: how the chocolate tasted, how it felt as it melted in your fingers, how the flavours stayed with you, and how it was gone before you knew what had happened, leaving you wanting more immediately.

I think we all have a wonderful memory of this kind, and I am going to share mine with you, as it was poignant and completely life-changing.

I don't recall the exact year – it was probably 1985 or 1986. My grandma's lounge was at the front of her bungalow, which my grandad had built in the fifties, and it looked out on to tall trees, open fields and amber-glowing street lights. It was Christmas Day, and dark by 3.30pm.

It was an uncluttered and tidy yet warm and comforting place to be, with festive excitement in the air mingling with a cosy tiredness that was beginning to creep in. I was kneeling on the shaggy yellow rug in front of the open coal fire, enjoying the heat of it on my back. My family was sitting around me, all too full after a huge Christmas lunch (and, of course, Christmas pudding), but we all still had room for festive sweets, nuts and chocolates. I was handed a box wrapped in Christmassy paper. I gave it a shake (I always shake a wrapped present, do you? So much fun guessing what's inside) and it rattled. I had no idea what it contained, so, as usual, I ripped off the paper in a hurry. Inside was a perfectly square box with gold foil-blocked decoration and 'Thorntons Continental' written across the top. I had always loved the sophisticated things it seemed only grown-ups could enjoy, like perfume, dressy shoes, styled hair and alcohol, so receiving a luxury box of chocolates swept me up in a tidal wave of feeling grown-up way beyond my years. Of course, I opened them immediately and took out the chocolate guide, exposing a crinkly-sounding gold tray beneath that held each chocolate in place. This is where the life-changing moment began. As I lifted the lid, the intense smells and aromas from the chocolates were overwhelming: vanilla, almonds, hazelnuts, sugar and chocolate, all mingled, muddled and mixed together, filling my entire head. And the names! I looked at the names of each chocolate as if they were those of people, friends and family. They had an identity. There was Alpini, a log of milk chocolate, almonds and hazelnuts, and the Diplomat, which was similar to the Alpini and quickly made me fall in love with something called praline. The Lemon Parfait was a light, whipped zingy filling with a dark chocolate shell, but the one I found most intriguing was the Viennese Truffle, with a crystalline sugar coating hiding a buttery melting truffle filling. I had seen nothing like this until now.

Grandma's for tea, enjoying marshmallows dipped in milk chocolate and crisped rice. I ate so many.

My stomach turned and churned as I realised I was probably supposed to hand this precious box around the room. I wanted nothing to do with sharing on this occasion. I wanted to experience every single one myself, and fall in love with each special chocolate. Strangely enough, I cannot recall what happened next or whether I was allowed to keep them all for myself, but the experience of opening that box and gazing at the contents changed how I looked at chocolates, as I began to understand how unique and special they could be. Chocolates like this were for special occasions only.

I've received many boxes for birthdays and Christmas since then, but this memory has always stayed close to the front of my mind. At the time, I had no ambitions of becoming a chocolatier. I simply knew I loved the luxurious textures, tastes and form of chocolates that were inspired by or came from Europe and especially Belgium. Do I still? Keep reading.

Love at first bite

The type of chocolate, whether a truffle, bar, snack or brownie, does in some way dictate how we approach it, how we open it and how we take the first, second and third bite. Its shape and size, for example, will automatically control how you enjoy that first taste. A large chocolate bar moulded into a tablet with breakable square chunky portions has unwritten instructions in its DNA: *Break me into a strip, then break off individual squares of me to enjoy and share.* So we do. Rarely would we simply bite into a chocolate bar of this type and just munch our way through. At the other end of the spectrum is the Cadbury Flake, a treat enjoyed by so many of us since childhood. Long and thin, and pretty messy to eat, this is a one-person, no-sharing chocolate bar, which adds to the ritual and experience. I'll delve into the racy advertising of the Cadbury Flake in chapter four, but for now let's look at how eating the Cadbury Flake became so unforgettable – and so flipping difficult. You cannot break it or cut it; ultimately, you can't really do anything other than manhandle it in a way that always looks somewhat sexual. It's incredibly crumbly, so you need both hands free and some pretty dynamic lips (and you should never wear white when eating a Cadbury Flake). It's a ritual: you sit down by yourself and carefully unpeel the wrapper, catching all the crumbly bits that have fallen off as it's been blundering around inside your bag or pocket getting broken and damaged. It may only have cost 60p, but you paid for it, and you are going to save every last piece of chocolate at risk of hitting the floor, getting stuck in your jumper or falling onto your chest to melt and get sticky. Then you bite it and enjoy that unforgettable milk chocolate flavour. You chew and allow it to melt, and before long – and after displaying some expert lip gymnastics and the reflexes of an athlete as you catch all the crumbs – you have finished. The chocolate flavour vanishes pretty quickly. It's not about a complex and intoxicating aftertaste, but more the enjoyable ritual of eating it and the comfort of tasting something nostalgic and reliable. Lovely, isn't it?

Did you know?
Chocolate tasting notes are not added ingredients, but intrinsic to the chocolate.

The difference between eating and tasting

Despite the undeniable joy of the kind of ritual I've just described, it's worth noting that *eating* chocolate and *tasting* chocolate are two very different things.

When you eat chocolate, you may not analyse each and every flavour and examine the complex nuances; often, we simply enjoy it (and eat it too quickly). There's no harm in that, especially when the enjoyment is so absolute and fulfilling (like when you're having a moment with a Cadbury Flake). However, when it comes to tasting fine chocolate, especially dark chocolate, a different approach should be adopted so you can feel and taste every part of the cacao beans' characters and complexities. It's an exciting process. In the beginning, you may find it a little overwhelming and complicated, but my advice is to simply trust your tongue, as only you will taste what you taste; what you experience is yours and only yours, so you cannot be wrong.

Slowing down our tasting of food, especially fine chocolate, can give you the most euphoric and pleasurable experience you can imagine. You could wolf down the very same piece of chocolate in a rush and lose the experience fully in your hurry for enjoyment. In the same breath, though, tasting chocolate in this slower way can also uncover some unpleasant tastes and flavours that might be trapped in your chocolate, so you need to be able to understand and identify what's good and what's not.

We all chew differently, we all taste differently, and we all enjoy our food differently. For example, I chew predominantly on my right-hand side and have to make an effort to move my food around my whole mouth to get all the flavours. Your normal way of eating is as important to consider when it comes to tasting as any formalised and structured tasting method.

Let's explore two different approaches to identifying the complexities in fine chocolate and how you can adopt these when it's your turn to start tasting.

Slowing down

So, how slow should you go when tasting chocolate? Someone who has spent over 20 years exploring and enjoying fine cacao and chocolate in detail is Martin Christy, co-founder of the International Institute of Chocolate and Cacao Tasting, and all-round chocolate expert. He has travelled the globe, reviewing and tasting chocolate, and awarding and supporting many cacao growers and chocolate producers. There is very little Martin doesn't know about tasting chocolate, and he has some really useful advice for anyone just starting out on this wonderful tasting journey.

When you first start tasting fine chocolate, you should take your time, Martin says. This allows you to experience all the complexities and nuances the chocolate has hidden within it, and to discover them in your own way. Taste the chocolate consciously and be alert to all the flavours you are experiencing. Ignore external distractions and noises while tasting, and try to focus on every part of the chocolate. Tasting fine chocolate is like learning a new language: there are words to describe what you are tasting and experiencing, but you may not be able to articulate them in the beginning. Just don't be afraid to say what you feel and what you taste. If the chocolate tastes chocolatey, then say it. You might think it's obvious, but it's not. In fact, some chocolate doesn't taste chocolatey.

When we are finding it hard to describe what we are experiencing, Martin explains that our faces can say more than our voices. For example, when you taste something you don't like, it's a split-second reaction that is expressed on your faces well before you say anything, as it takes two seconds for your brain to actually identify the taste or understand what it is you dislike about it. So trust yourself and what you are experiencing. You own your tongue, so what you are tasting is unique to you. You may like the chocolate and you may not, and either one is absolutely OK.

The International Institute of Chocolate and Cacao Tasting offers accredited courses that work through progressively challenging stages to teach students how to taste cacao and chocolate to a highly sophisticated level. It takes a serious amount of studying, tasting and time, and you need to really understand your own taste experience to pass each course. Martin explains that the institute adopts a formalised approach to chocolate tasting. First of all, chocolate is not a staple food; we eat it for pleasure, and we can survive without it, unlike many other foodstuffs. (We both laughed when he told me that, as we both agreed that we think a lot of us could *not* survive without chocolate!)

Pleasure is subjective, Martin told me, and so is tasting, so it's important to embrace this when teaching students how to start tasting chocolate. Tasting more slowly is something Martin encourages, because when you eat fine cacao chocolate quickly, not only will you lose the complexities and nuances within the chocolate, but you are also likely to experience the tannins as a more prominent taste, resulting in a chocolate that tastes more bitter.

Slowing down gives you, your tongue and your brain the opportunity to identify, analyse and experience everything the chocolate has to offer, even if this is something you dislike. Try it for yourself, but remember this approach is for tasting fine chocolate. Commercial chocolate made by multinational companies will not have the delicate complexities suspended within it.

Tasting with colour

Another approach that really caught my eye comes from food scientist and chocolate lover Hazel Lee. Hazel visited her first cacao plantation while on holiday in 2014, and this experience significantly increased her already existing fascination with and love for chocolate.

Like many of us, Hazel has sometimes found it difficult to articulate what she was tasting in chocolate, so she has created a unique and original tool to help. It's called Taste with Colour, it can be found here: hazeljlee.com/taste-with-colour/. It's a wonderful, colourful chart where different hues represent particular flavours, for example the colours green and all its shades reference flavours including basil, green tea, apple and grassy.

Hazel's approach to tasting is less formal, and Hazel doesn't claim to have used any particular scientific evidence when developing this method – she just devised something to help herself, and then realised it could also help others. Hazel believes passionately that we own our own taste. No one can ever say that you are wrong for tasting what you taste, no matter what the chocolate wrapper or anyone else says.

Always taste blind, as even the wrapper design from a bar of chocolate can influence what you are going to taste. For example, if a bar of chocolate has an orange wrapper, then we are hard-wired to think of orangey and zesty flavours; the same goes for the colour green and minty or herbal flavours.

When you're ready to taste your chocolate, take a square or two and place it at the side of the chart, then put it in your mouth. Close your eyes and, as soon as you start tasting, try to see the colour of that taste in your mind's eye. Treat it like a kind of meditation. Open your eyes and look at the chart, seeking out the colour you have just experienced, then write it down.

I tried this method when tasting a Madagascan 64 per cent chocolate. My immediate taste was mouth-watering astringency and a vibrant red – not deep red or burgundy, but a bright, summery red, followed at the end by some similarly vibrant yellow and orange colours. Happy chocolate, I like to call it. Looking at Hazel's chart, the colours I had experienced gave me the following flavour names: raspberry, cherry, fruity, passion fruit and tropical fruits. Now, I already know that Madagascan chocolate is going to be fruity and mouth-watering, but all chocolate is different and has different levels of flavour. Hazel's method of tasting is actually already hard-wired into our brains, as we all know which foods are green, yellow or orange, but her chart helps us to articulate this clearly in confident tasting notes.

One of my favourite things about Hazel's approach is that she also uses painting in her tastings, and the results from different participants can be very surprising. Once you have tasted and discovered your colours, you use a piece of paper to paint the 'waves of taste', allowing you to express which are stronger and which are more delicate, and show what stands out for you and how your mind sees your tasting experience. You don't need to be an artist for this. Just take it page by page in a new

Did you know?
You should never eat chocolate straight from the fridge. It's too cold and will alter the melting experience in the mouth, resulting in a distorted tasting experience. Taste at room temperature only. Avoid storing chocolate in the fridge at all. If you have very hot weather and it's at risk of melting, you can refrigerate, but always allow it to come up to room temperature in the sealed wrapper before tasting.

notebook – now your chocolate tasting book – and build up a personal tasting library. You could attach the empty chocolate bar wrapper to each page and see if your colours align with the chocolate maker's packaging and description on the chocolate. Remember, though, there's no need to feel demotivated if you don't agree with the tasting notes printed on chocolate bar wrapper. This is about your tongue, your taste, your mind and your experience.

Chocolate is meant to be enjoyed, so if one of your pages doesn't give you joy and has colours you don't like, then although you will still benefit from understanding the complexities and balance of the chocolate, it may also show you that you didn't actually like it, and don't want to eat it again.

Emotional tasting

From a professional point of view, it's important for me to look at how my suppliers taste the chocolate that I use in my creations. When you buy anything made with chocolate from a chocolatier like myself, you are also buying the chocolate the producer made, which will hold all those exciting flavours and complexities the producer has worked so hard to develop. In order to create my own products, I have to decide which origin or blended chocolate to use, and it helps to examine the producer's tasting tools, which they have spent significant time researching and investing in. One of my suppliers is the French company Valrhona, who have created a chocolate-tasting guide to help identify those all-important flavours. Interestingly, the guide includes the emotions we may experience when tasting the chocolates, not just the tastes and flavours.

Did you know?
There are up to 800 taste and flavour compounds you can detect in fine chocolate.

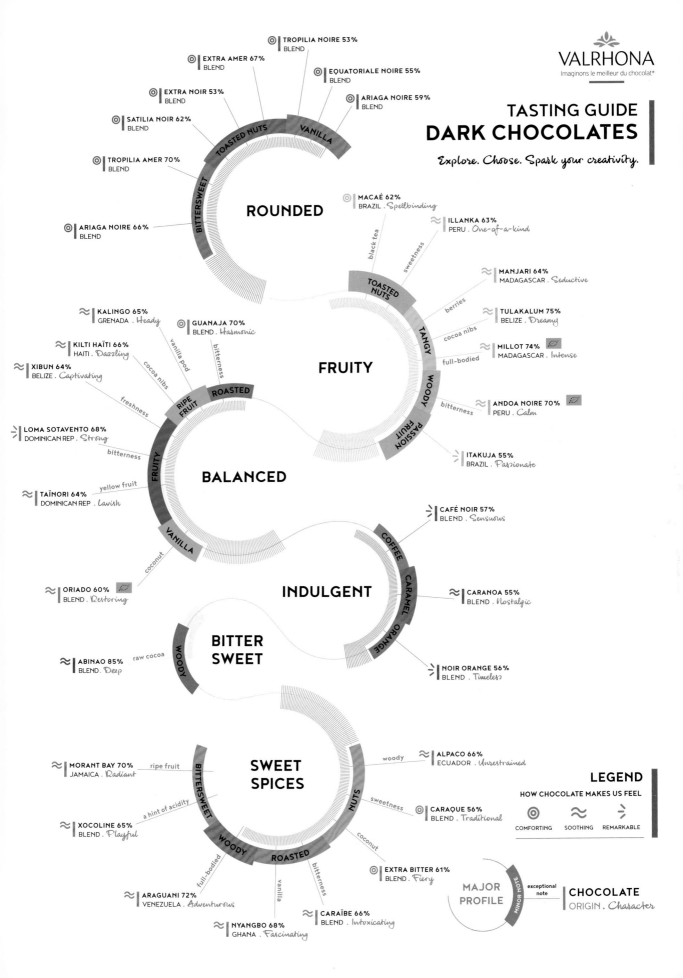

VALRHONA
Imaginons le meilleur du chocolat®

TASTING GUIDE
DARK CHOCOLATES

Explore. Choose. Spark your creativity.

TROPILIA NOIRE 53%
BLEND

EXTRA AMER 67%
BLEND

EQUATORIALE NOIRE 55%
BLEND

EXTRA NOIR 53%
BLEND

ARIAGA NOIRE 59%
BLEND

SATILIA NOIR 62%
BLEND

TROPILIA AMER 70%
BLEND

ARIAGA NOIRE 66%
BLEND

ROUNDED

TOASTED NUTS

VANILLA

BITTERSWEET

MACAÉ 62%
BRAZIL . *Spellbinding*

ILLANKA 63%
PERU . *One-of-a-kind*

black tea

sweetness

TOASTED
NUTS

MANJARI 64%
MADAGASCAR . *Seductive*

berries

TANGY

TULAKALUM 75%
BELIZE . *Dreamy*

cocoa nibs

FRUITY

MILLOT 74%
MADAGASCAR . *Intense*

full-bodied

WOODY

ANDOA NOIRE 70%
PERU . *Calm*

bitterness

PASSION FRUIT

KALINGO 65%
GRENADA . *Heady*

GUANAJA 70%
BLEND . *Harmonic*

KILTI HAÏTI 66%
HAÏTI . *Dazzling*

vanilla pod

bitterness

XIBUN 64%
BELIZE . *Captivating*

cocoa nibs

freshness

ROASTED

RIPE
FRUIT

ITAKUJA 55%
BRAZIL . *Passionate*

LOMA SOTAVENTO 68%
DOMINICAN REP . *Strong*

bitterness

FRUITY

BALANCED

TAÎNORI 64%
DOMINICAN REP . *Lavish*

yellow fruit

VANILLA

CAFÉ NOIR 57%
BLEND . *Sensuous*

COFFEE

coconut

CARAMEL

ORIADO 60%
BLEND . *Restoring*

INDULGENT

CARANOA 55%
BLEND . *Nostalgic*

ORANGE

BITTER
SWEET

WOODY

ABINAO 85%
BLEND . *Deep*

raw cocoa

NOIR ORANGE 56%
BLEND . *Timeless*

MORANT BAY 70%
JAMAICA . *Radiant*

ripe fruit

BITTERSWEET

SWEET
SPICES

ALPACO 66%
ECUADOR . *Unrestrained*

woody

NUTS

sweetness

CARAQUE 56%
BLEND . *Traditional*

XOCOLINE 65%
BLEND . *Playful*

a hint of acidity

WOODY

coconut

LEGEND

HOW CHOCOLATE MAKES US FEEL

COMFORTING   SOOTHING   REMARKABLE

ROASTED

EXTRA BITTER 61%
BLEND . *Fiery*

bitterness

full-bodied

vanilla

ARAGUANI 72%
VENEZUELA . *Adventurous*

CARAÏBE 66%
BLEND . *Intoxicating*

NYANGBO 68%
GHANA . *Fascinating*

MAJOR
PROFILE

MINOR NOTE

exceptional
note

CHOCOLATE
ORIGIN . *Character*

How to hold your own chocolate tasting

Now it's your turn to have your own chocolate tasting, as you have all the skills and information to discover the mesmerising flavours, tastes and textures in both the chocolate you already love and the chocolate you are about to discover. Remember, I'm not asking you to taste confectionery, but fine milk and dark chocolate, chocolate made without any vegetable fats and artificial ingredients.

It's impossible for me to list every bean variety and type of chocolate; however, my guide below will help you navigate your way through different types of cacao and chocolate, the various origins that are available in chocolate shops and supermarkets, and, of course, blended chocolate, where you are likely to taste the producer's characteristics within the chocolate rather than the individual bean character. For example, take Lindt dark chocolate. As it is mass produced for the world marketplace, it needs to be the same every time. For me, its character is heavily bitter with quite a lot of vanilla and sweetness in the aftertaste, but it's hard to identify the delicate nuances of a particular cacao bean character.

So, where do you find the chocolate I'm talking about, with all of the fine-tasting characters and complexities? We are so lucky to be able to buy pretty much anything online these days, including not just mass-produced chocolate, but also micro-batch or craft chocolate. Even our supermarkets now stock single-origin milk and dark chocolate. Finding interesting chocolate to taste and enjoy isn't too difficult. Buy a variety of different origins, blends and percentages, and include some mainstream dark chocolate too, so you can compare the vast difference between them.

This might all sound a little overwhelming, but I've prepared the tasting table opposite to guide you through it. You can simply scan it and print out to use over and over again.

Preparing for your tasting

- Start by selecting your chocolate. Arrange pieces of the chocolate in order of percentage, and put the milk and dark chocolate into two separate piles.
- Using my table opposite, fill in the relevant information from the chocolate bar wrappers, then put the bar wrappers away, out of sight.
- Make sure your chocolate has not been refrigerated. Room temperature is always best.
- Have glasses of water ready and either some water crackers or apple slices to neutralise your palate between tastings.

Chocolate maker/ producer	Origin/Blend	Cacao %	Flavours and tastes	Texture	Aromas	Score 1 to 10 (1 being loathe and 10 being love)

EATING CHOCOLATE AND THE ETIQUETTE OF TASTING

How do you eat yours?

You may recognise this question from Cadbury Creme Egg adverts. The campaign really caught the public imagination, so much so that social media posts on the topic were rife, and we started to ask the question whenever we saw someone eating a Creme Egg. It was a clever and inventive advert, as it tapped into our eating rituals and the ways in which we enjoy eating our everyday chocolate.

As important as tasting is, there is a great deal of joy in the simple eating of chocolate, and I don't want to overlook that. As I explained in my musings on the Cadbury Flake on page 38, I've always loved the rituals we each build around how we enjoy our chocolate. They can be small things, some of which are entirely unique to you, and others as we all do, which only strengthens our sense of chocolate that something we have all fallen in love with worldwide.

When I was very young, five or six years old, I remember sitting on my mum's knee. It must have been Christmas or a birthday, as we had a tin of chocolates. We also had one of two very famous tins of chocolates on special occasions: Quality Street® or Cadbury Roses. I was 100 per cent a Roses kid. I loved the selection, with my go-tos being the Hazelnut Swirl and the Tangy Orange Creme. However, on this occasion it was Quality Street® we were digging in to. My mum had a particular way of eating her chocolates that I found so fun and clever. She used to smooth out each foil wrapper perfectly on the arm of the chair, taking great care not to rip or crease it. Within a few minutes, she would have formed it into a perfectly sculpted wine glass or goblet. They were so delicate and beautiful, and I loved watching her make them. In a way, the chocolate inside was secondary to what we could make from the foil wrapper. I still do this today with any foil-wrapped chocolate. And don't think the colourful see-through plastic chocolate wrappers were forgotten about. Definitely not: these were always held up to our eyes so we could experience the world in vivid, green, red, yellow and purple. The colourful joy of doing this still makes me smile even today; it's always so much fun to see the world in a psychedelic mix of colours.

The act of unwrapping chocolate can be as satisfying as eating it. Perhaps the most famous example is the KitKat®, with its very thin but super-shiny foil wrapper with the iconic red paper belly band around it. There was only one way to open it, and we'd all been trained how to do it by the TV adverts. You'd remove the paper, then hold the bar firmly and (if you hadn't bitten your thumbnail down to the quick) could slice through the foil between two fingers of chocolate and snap the first finger off the bar. I loved doing this so much, and I get the same satisfying feeling when I am the one to plunge my teaspoon through the tight foil seal of a coffee jar. Oh, the joy!

Did you know?
Several of the big names in chocolate today (Cadbury, Fry, Rowntree) are companies founded by Quaker families.

And then comes the ritual of eating the KitKat®. Despite the fact we all open them in the same way, I've discovered, through many conversations over many years, that there are a number of different ways of eating them. The most common way is to begin by biting off each end. The reason? To find out if you are one of the lucky 'winners' that gets a stick of solid chocolate and no wafer. Now, I've never understood the excitement around this, as I *love* wafers; I would have more wafers if it was possible. The second most common ritual is to bite off all the chocolate from the sides, nibbling away like a food-hoarding hamster until the wafer is exposed – definitely less inviting, in my opinion. I favour the third KitKat-eating ritual, which I follow whether it's a two-finger or four-finger bar, or even a KitKat Chunky®, and regardless of flavour. You will need either a glass of whole milk, or a mug of milky tea or milky coffee. Bite off each end of the chocolate, then use the stick of KitKat® as a straw and dip one end into your drink. Suck the other end really hard until the liquid has flooded the wafer and hits your tongue. Now stop and allow the wafer to soften slightly before eating. If you use tea or coffee, then you have the extra joy of the chocolate melting slightly too: pure ecstasy. The last way of enjoying a KitKat®, and the one the manufacturer recommends, is simply to snap off a finger and eat it, so that every mouthful is a harmonious blend of both chocolate and wafer. Whichever way you have adopted, that's your way of heightening your enjoyment of a familiar favourite.

Eating dark chocolate

Dark chocolate of any variety always gives off an air of superiority. This begins when we are very young, with our parents and anyone of adult age saying, 'Dark chocolate isn't for children, it's for grown-ups. It's too bitter; you won't like it.' Now, anything grown-ups have, kids automatically want, and if they say you won't like it, then you want to try it even more. I did try it, and remember liking it, but it was likely to have been Cadbury Bournville, which has a very low cocoa percentage for a dark chocolate.

Dark chocolate has a more intense and intoxicating taste and flavour that really fills our taste buds and stays with us after we have swallowed – surprisingly, the taste can linger for up to 30 minutes after we have finished it. This means we tend to eat it more slowly, and we are more likely to have just a square or two and keep the rest for another day, unlike milk and white chocolate, which we tend to wolf down more quickly. Because of this, our rituals with dark chocolate are a bit more considered. Many people enjoy just one or two squares every evening after dinner, and that's enough. Without us consciously realising it, this approach makes the chocolate feel more precious, as we are deciding to enjoy it over a long period and not just in one go. Now, I'm not saying there is a right or wrong way

to enjoy chocolate, as we are all very different, but this tendency to take our time with dark chocolate is very common, and I find it so interesting that we treat milk and dark chocolate differently.

I differ from the pack slightly here, because if I have one square of dark chocolate and I love it, then I'm eating the whole bar in one day, not stretching it out over a few days. If I fall in love, then I want a full-on passionate relationship. I want to taste it all – and I'm not sharing. I have a rule, though, that I never eat dark chocolate after 6pm unless I'm at dinner or hosting a chocolate event, as I really cannot sleep after eating dark chocolate.

When I chatted with Martin Christy (see page 39), we also discussed how each of us eat a chocolate truffle or a filled chocolate, as there isn't a right or wrong way. Or is there? Well, it all comes down to the type of truffle or filled chocolate it is. We agreed that a liqueur-filled chocolate has to be eaten in one enjoyable bite – you know the ones, they usually have a spirit-based sugary syrup filling, like whisky or brandy, and are popular at Christmas time. I absolutely loved these growing up, and even as a young boy, my Christmas stocking would contain a mini box of Famous Names Signature Collection liqueurs, ready for me to find in the early hours of Christmas morning. I think we've all attempted to bite into these kinds of chocolates, only to have the filling spill down our clothes. So pop it in and enjoy the boozy warmth, and then allow the chocolate to melt. You either love or hate this type of chocolate. (I'll let you in on a little secret – thanks to my rather mischievous Father Christmas, I still love them, and I actually ordered a box online to enjoy while writing this book. #JoyJoyJoy.)

A truffle – well, an authentic truffle – is a blend of cream and dark chocolate, hand-rolled and dusted with cocoa powder, They are the most luxurious and sexy chocolate of all. What can come close to sinking your teeth into silky ganache, with the way it immediately starts to melt and become velvety, so that you barely need to chew or even swallow? You need a private moment to really enjoy these. Let me give you a little advice: next time you have a date night or a spot of seduction planned, make my recipe for Dark Chocolate Truffles (page 164). Trust me, they work *very* well: before, during and after. So, do you bite these or pop the entire truffle in to enjoy it? I say do both. Bite the first one in half to see the filling, to smell and experience it, then for your second, third and fourth, pop the entire thing in and allow it to melt away. Close your eyes and simply enjoy this very special chocolate.

Did you know?
Your memories and understanding of where you are in the world, what you eat and what you have available to you all directly influence how you experience taste and flavour, and how you express what you are tasting to others.

Craft or micro-batch chocolate

A global phenomenon: that's the only way I can describe the exciting growth of craft or micro-batch chocolate since 2008. The boom is unrivalled: never before have we seen so many new bean-to-bar makers popping up in all corners of the globe. It's wonderful to see so much joy and passion for what once was a very challenging business to get into. That's all changed, and is still changing.

The term 'craft chocolate' is pretty new, but it has caught on very quickly, and is used to define small-batch bean-to-bar, tree-to-bar or blossom-to-bar, chocolate making. Craft chocolate producers often source their cacao beans from smaller plantations or growers, then roast, grind, conch, temper and mould their bars themselves in-house. Thanks to these makers, we are seeing more exclusive and limited-edition chocolate bars, with so many origins and varieties of chocolate, as they can buy beans in smaller quantities from plantation growers that do not supply the multinational companies. Craft chocolate is such a great way to support smaller cacao plantation growers.

In this chapter we'll explore how craft chocolate has changed the chocolate scene forever; how it drew people away from their day jobs into new careers; how consumers have reacted to chocolate bars that cost as much as a bottle of good wine; and the impact the movement has had on the growers themselves.

What is craft chocolate?

So, what is micro-batch, bean-to-bar, tree-to-bar or craft chocolate? I first heard these now commonly used terms in 2009, when I heard rumours about a new company, that was run and owned by two brothers who were making chocolate in small batches, from the bean. People said it was a new character and style of chocolate. Mast Brothers is based in Williamsburg, Brooklyn. Their style was new and fresh, and not something we'd seen before in the UK, although it's since become more familiar: think filament bulbs, bare brick walls, lots of natural surfaces, robust, utilitarian fabrics, craft materials and handmade paper wrappers. They had very much adopted an old-school methodology and style. The brothers, Michael and Rik, even honed their personal styles to absolutely represent their business and vision. They lived and breathed it. I found it not just fascinating, but also so comfortable and slightly nostalgic. The smell in their Williamsburg space was deliciously intoxicating, and one I had not experienced much in my time as a chocolatier. The roasting of cacao beans is unmistakable: spicy, aromatic, heady and joyous to everyone who smells it. It's a winning formula. It says: *We make our chocolate here, and you can buy it here, and it's beautifully hand-moulded and hand-wrapped in wrappers we designed and printed.* It was new and inspiring – so much so, that we started selling their chocolate in our shops. Our 'supply chain' was my business partner filling up suitcases when visiting New York and bringing the chocolate home.

The brothers' passion was addictive and catching, and it wasn't long before we organised an event with Mast Brothers in Brooklyn when I launched my first book, *Adventures with Chocolate*. I have the most wonderful and emotional memories of this time. What made it even more special was that I was with my very best friend, Kate, who shares my obsession with chocolate, Williamsburg and its then-new movement of style and creativity – oh, and the amazing food that infused the air, along with whisperings of the latest openings we had to try. This was the first time I had experienced queuing to get into a restaurant – and I mean waiting an hour or more because the food was so incredible. The hour-long waits were worth it, though. I cannot tell you how much this small chapter in my life inspired me and still does; it's impossible to put into words, but I felt the happiest I'd ever been, and I often revisit my memories of this time when I'm feeling creatively challenged and overwhelmed by life. Chocolate does this. It takes you to places you would never usually have visited or experienced. It's a very emotional thing: talk to any chocolate maker and they will get emotional and passionate as they talk from the heart about their journey.

The process of making craft chocolate

So, how do the processes involved in chocolate-making differ when done on a small craft scale?

You will recognise some of the processes from my chat with Gary Guittard (page 23), however the size of refining equipment and manpower is very different when making in small batches.

Someone I know well who explains the process brilliantly is Phil Landers of Land Chocolate. Phil started his chocolate career as a sales assistant for me. He then went on to work with Mast Brothers to learn the bean-to-bar process, before opening his own bean-to-bar chocolate production in Hackney, London. I asked Phil to explain the process, from the beans arriving to the finished bar of craft chocolate.

At Land, my job as chocolate maker is to highlight the nuances and flavour notes of the cacao beans, which have been carefully developed by the cacao farmers at origin. I do this by tweaking the manufacturing process to suit each individual batch and fully nurture the flavour potential of the cacao bean every time.

Once the beans have been delivered, I hand-sort them. For each batch of chocolate, depending on the cacao percentage of the bar, we'll sort through 30–45kg (66–90lb) of beans. This process involves removing spoiled beans and any foreign materials; sometimes we find the odd dead bug stowaway who came along for the ride from the farm.

Next, we roast! Now, it's important to point out that roasting is not a one-size-fits-all process; there are many different approaches. At Land, we sit in the middle: favouring equal parts scientific precision, trial and error and trusting the senses of taste and smell (the best part). Every bean variety has its own distinct personality, so we have developed a different roasting profile for each, ranging from anywhere between 15 and 35 minutes, but all done in a rather basic yet lovable 5kg (11lb) convection oven.

Now it's time for cracking and winnowing. For those of you who don't know, the object of this step is to crack open the beans and discard the unwanted husks, which at Land takes place on a rather primitive device I put together with my dad (there may have been tears; the less said, the better). It's a bespoke hybrid of second-hand machines and a household hoover that successfully cracks open the beans and blows away the husks, leaving us with 20–30kg (40–66lb) of clean cacao nib ready to load up into the melangeur (a cacao bean grinder that takes cacao nibs from solid to liquid) and turn into chocolate. On a good day, this will take 3 to 4 hours. If only every day was a good day.

We then grind the nibs in a rather traditional stone granite melangeur, leaving the nibs and sugar to grind away and liquify for at least 72 hours. Over time, particle size reduces to something between 15–20 microns, something that feels smooth on the tongue. Finally, we're approaching something that resembles the chocolate we know and love. The now 50kg (110lb) of chocolate is moved from the grinder to the conche. Here, we do some final flavour development, which involves agitating the chocolate to improve mouthfeel, drive off any leftover volatile acids and coax out the deeper, more nuanced flavour notes. The chocolate then sits and ages for a couple of weeks before being tempered and finally hand-wrapped.

One batch of Land Chocolate produces about 700–800 bars, and all in all, takes about 5 to 6 days.

In some people's world, that is a lot of chocolate, but in the chocolate industry, it's a mere dot on the horizon … a very tasty dot.

The price

Price is something I'm asked about so often with craft chocolate. Yes, it's expensive compared to mainstream chocolate bars, and yes, it *should* be expensive: it has to be, so that the cacao growers are paid well and fairly. Expect to pay anything from £5–10 per 75g (2¾oz) bar for craft chocolate, and sometimes more if it's very rare small-batch chocolate. If you feel this is overpriced, then I want you to understand that chocolate is too cheap, and has been for decades – so cheap that many growers around the world get paid significantly below the poverty line for their cacao beans. Most micro-batch makers are paying the right price for the beans: a higher price, because they are supporting the growers directly, meaning the growers can invest in themselves, their trees, their workers and their families. Chocolate is worth it. It's similar to buying wine: there are very cheap bottles out there that are neither complex nor interesting, with little to no story of the vineyard or the growers; and there's wine that has the story, the vintage and the variety, and is made by a producer who you know is doing good within the wine industry. When you buy from a craft bean-to-bar maker, you are often supporting the grower directly and making a small difference. Paying up to £10 for a bar of chocolate means it's special: you consider every piece you put on your tongue and enjoy everything it has to bring. It's an experience worth every cacao bean it is made with.

Some of my favourite craft bars

It would be impossible to name every micro-batch/craft chocolate maker now in existence, so I will name some of my favourites who I feel have really made an impact on me over the last 15-year period. When I say they made an impact on me, what I really mean is that they have made chocolate that has stayed with me, and that as well as their stunning chocolate, I have been impressed by their branding, sourcing and support for the growers. I also mean that simply eating their chocolate has made memories for me. I feel things very intensely, which some people say makes me a very sensitive person. I guess I am. I'm also a reflective thinker, so I have to work hard at being present, but when I taste a craft chocolate that makes time stand still, that has an immediate effect on my whole body and mind, then I know I'm in the present, and that something absolutely joyous has happened.

Did you know?
In 1994 Green & Black's Maya Gold chocolate bar became the first Fairtrade-certified product in the UK.

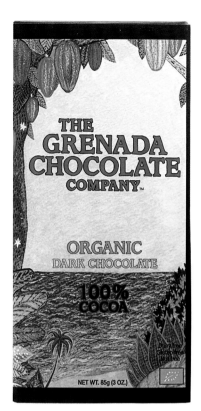

The Grenada Chocolate Company's bars (above) feature the vibrant colours of their plantation in the Caribbean, where they create farm-to-bar chocolate.

A craft chocolate bar from Dandelion Chocolate in San Francisco (opposite). Intoxicating, vibrant, unforgettable.

The Grenada Chocolate Company Craft chocolate is predominantly made many thousands of miles from its origin. Rarely is it made by the growers. But Mott Green, a trailblazer in the chocolate industry, started the Grenada Chocolate Company in 1999 with a pretty radical idea. The farmers growing the cacao beans could also make them into chocolate in small batches close to the farm. It meant there was no shipping of beans across the world to be processed into chocolate far from its origin. This idea of making chocolate on the farm was revolutionary back in 1999, and it's still not commonplace now, as it's a very challenging environment, with high heat and humidity to contend with, which cacao beans love, but all chocolate hates. I've had the joy of visiting the farm and small factory twice, and the aroma of fermenting and roasting cacao beans is wonderful. Sadly, Mott passed away in 2013, leaving us his legacy of passion, drive and determination to make amazing chocolate on the farm.

The chocolate made by the Grenada Chocolate Company is completely organic and grown over 150 acres, with raw cane sugar added for a delicate sweetness. The bars are packed with soft fruit flavours and are low in tannins, with a long finish of robust cacao and richness. This chocolate is a pure joy to eat. I must also mention that the factory is powered by solar energy, and the packaging is made from 50 per cent recycled and 25 per cent post-consumer-waste stock, and printed with vegetable inks.

Amano Chocolate One of the very first craft chocolates I ever tasted, this was created by Art Pollard in the Utah Valley in the US. Art uses ancient and modern techniques to create very individual-tasting chocolate that is packed with impact and character. The Amano bar that really moved me is their 70% Guayas. It's made using an Ecuadorian bean called Arriba, and it has all my favourite characters in it: cedar, smoke, molasses and blackberry. There's also a green banana character in there. Usually, I hate the taste of green banana, but with all the other complex characters present, it's balanced so well that, for me, it's not the most prominent flavour.

Dick Taylor Created by Adam Dick and Dustin Taylor in Northern California, this chocolate is made in distinctive bar moulds with incredibly intricate designs that make it a real joy visually. The bar that blew me away, and still does, is their 75% Brazil, with beans sourced directly from the growers Cacao Bahia. No vanilla is used in the production, just cacao beans and cane sugar, meaning its complex, unfiltered flavours are intense and robust, earthy and nutty – all characteristics I love in dark chocolate.

Dandelion Chocolate This company is based in San Francisco with a stunning production space in the Mission District where you can see the beans being roasted and ground. One bar really stands out for me: their Costa Esmeraldas 85%, from Ecuador. It's robust, strong and toasty, with a buttermilk tang. It's so full of vibrancy and flavour, and pairs perfectly with a fine single malt whisky.

Mast Brothers As I've said, the very first craft chocolate I had ever tasted was from Mast Brothers. It was like nothing else I had tasted before. It had a texture that was sandier than I was used to, and an intensity that blew my taste buds into outer space. Their Dominican Republic dark chocolate was so intense and full-flavoured that I must have eaten at least a bar a week for some time. Unfortunately, Mast Brothers have moved away from making single-origin chocolates, so this bar is no longer available.

Land Chocolate I can proudly say that Phil, who we met on page 53, was once an employee of mine, and clearly showed a true passion for all things chocolate. Now making his own craft chocolate in east London, UK, his 65% Honduras Malt bar is outstanding, with a deep long flavour and a maltiness from barley grain that makes it a very addictive eat.

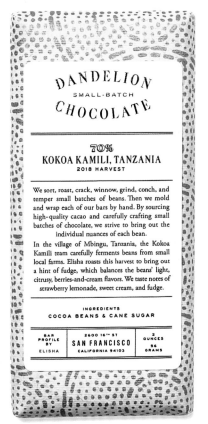

Dormouse Chocolates Isobel Carse was the very first craft chocolate maker in Manchester, UK, and has won numerous awards for her bean-to-bar chocolate. It's what I like to call very honest chocolate: chocolate where every bar is wonderful and lots of great care has gone into the development and roasting of the beans. The standout bar for me is the 71.5% Kablon Farm, The Philippines dark chocolate. It has toasted oats in its character, along with some tropical fruits and an astringency that I love.

Bare Bones In May 2020, I bought a bar of Dominican Republic 68% Sea Salt Chocolate from these makers, who are based in Glasgow, Scotland. It was the most wonderful bar of chocolate I had tasted in years, with a balanced, light and gentle roast, and exactly the right amount of sea salt and crisp. Time stopped; my day was a better because of this bar of chocolate. As you will hear me say throughout the book, chocolate can take you to places you never thought you would go. This one took me to a very happy place at a time when I really needed that happy place to go to.

FireTree It's so good, it's volcanic – literally, as all the chocolate is made with cacao beans grown in volcanic soils, predominantly from the Solomon Islands region but with some from Madagascar and The Philippines too. Based in Peterborough, UK, when I first tasted FireTree chocolate, it was the texture that really struck me as special. It's the perfect smoothness and viscosity for a very satisfying eat, and the taste is incredibly earthy with a mineral finish and an incredibly complex aftertaste. I cannot pick just one, as they are all magical.

Original Beans Philipp Kauffmann, who is based in the Netherlands, started growing and making chocolate in 2008, and the bar he gave me to try was an origin I had never sampled before: Virunga 70%, made with beans from the Virunga National Park in the east of the Democratic Republic of the Congo. It's deeply earthy, yet very easy to enjoy as it's so well balanced, with no bitterness or harsh tannins. The aftertaste is of black tea and very ripe black cherry skins.

Pacari You can't buy a more ethical chocolate, period, than that made by Ecuadorian producers Pacari. This is true of any of their chocolate bars, but it's the 70% Raw that really blows me away, as it's incredibly fragrant and has all the character of the Nacional cacao bean, which I truly love. There is an ease to this chocolate that allows it to be enjoyed at any time of the day or night, and its aftertaste is so long and delicate that I find I eat it very quickly while still enjoying every complex nuance it delivers.

Craft chocolate makers have changed the way we eat and buy chocolate in so many ways, and visually this could not be more apparent. BCC (Before Craft Chocolate), we had mainstream chocolate bars with wrappers that were familiar in terms of look, materials and messaging: all very generic and safe. Then craft chocolate makers flipped this on its head and introduced wrappers that were individually designed and printed, with textural papers, dazzling foils and innovative ways to seal the chocolate bar. Mast Brothers were trailblazers, and their wrappers have been copied by many, and inspired many more. It was their simplicity that won consumers over: thick papers, designs that were the brothers' own inventions, and a simple paper sticker to seal, with just enough information about the bar. It was such a simple and old-school way of presenting a chocolate bar, and people loved it. It wasn't new – it called back to the days before plastic wrappers, updating traditional packaging and presenting it in a way that we all felt somehow attached to. A wonderful source of further information about craft chocolate and its makers (as well as a generously stocked online shop) is Cocoa Runners (cocoarunners.com). I signed up for their monthly subscription, so I receive four craft chocolate bars from many different producers each month so I can learn about these wonderful varieties of chocolate. The website has an online library of information, and their email

Did you know?
It takes approximately 600 cacao beans to make 450g (1lb) chocolate – that's around 12–14 cacao pods.

newsletters are packed full of fantastic facts about so many subjects, from taste and diet to chocolate making and what exactly is a truffle? Their Chocopedia is fantastic: if you have a question about fine chocolate, you'll find the answer there. It's a must-visit place if you love craft chocolate.

Making your own bean-to-bar chocolate

The recipes and methods in this chapter will show you how to make chocolate at home from the cacao bean, and how to use your homemade chocolate.

There is no better way to experience micro-batch chocolate than to have a go at making your own. It's time-consuming and labour-intensive, and so worth it, just to taste your very own handmade, homemade chocolate. You will get a lot of joy from this process, and it will make you very happy when you take your first bite.

You will need a few basic tools to get started: a hairdryer, an oven, a granite or stone pestle and mortar, a digital thermometer, a palette knife, a scraper, a timer and the most important tool of all, your hands.

Ingredients to make cocoa mass or cocoa liquor (100 per cent cocoa solids chocolate)

- dried cacao beans of a blend or origin of your choice. 100g (3½oz) dried beans will yield 75–85g (2½–3oz) of cocoa mass/liquor.

Ingredients to make 70 per cent dark chocolate

- cocoa mass or cocoa liquor (7:3 ratio with sugar)
- unrefined cane sugar
- cocoa butter (optional – if your liquor is very thick and heavy, then adding cocoa butter will make it more fluid)

The stages

There are five stages to turning your beans into a bar of chocolate:

1. Roasting
2. Shelling and winnowing
3. Grinding
4. Sweetening your cocoa mass
5. Tempering

We'll begin by making the cocoa mass or liquor, which is the basis of all milk and dark chocolate bars.

Roasting

It's so important to roast the beans to kill any harmful bacteria caused in the fermentation process, especially those that may have been picked up from the ground, where many beans are dried (see page 21).

I'm very aware that other chocolate makers may suggest different temperatures and times for roasting, as there is no standardised time or temperature to get the perfect bean roast. I'm sharing the method that works best for me.

Preheat the oven to 140°C/120°C fan/275°F/gas 1. Place 2 clean baking trays in the oven to preheat.

Sort the beans by taking out anything that is not a bean (for example twigs, stones, etc.), and take out any gnarly twisted beans too. It's very important to wash your hands thoroughly after handling unroasted cacao beans. Get into this good habit to avoid any cross-contamination from the beans to you, your house or your family.

Lay the sorted beans in a single layer on your baking trays and roast in the oven for 15 minutes.

Remove the roasted beans from the oven and leave to cool.

Peel off the shell of one of the beans and taste the inside. Does it have a rounded, toasted flavour all the way through? Do you want a stronger roast? Or should you have given it less time in the oven for a more delicate roast? This is the exciting part, as you're deciding the character of your roast. Just remember to write everything down as you go so you can refer back to it later.

Shelling and winnowing

Winnowing means to separate the shell from the seed. I find this process very satisfying and therapeutic, as it takes time and patience. Press each bean to crack it open and peel off the outer shell, discarding it. You can do this individually or crush a few at a time. Once you have done this with all the beans, grab your hairdryer. Take a handful of the shelled and cracked beans from the baking tray and hold it over a bowl. With your other hand, switch on the hairdryer. Release the beans gradually so that they beans fall through the blast of air from the hairdryer on their way to the bowl. Any remaining lighter shell pieces will blow away from the heavier bean pieces as they fall. This is messy, so have a vacuum cleaner at the ready.

Repeat the process until you have separated the beans from the shells as much as possible.

Grinding

You will be pleased to know that there are now many cacoa bean melangeurs or grinders available to buy on the internet, but before you commit, a great way of seeing if you like making your own chocolate is to use a stone pestle and mortar. It's slow, yes, and you have to work in small batches, but honestly, I think it's worth the effort – and if you have family and friends to help, then even better.

You will need your hairdryer again, or a heat gun, the type used to strip paint from door frames.

Place some of the shelled cacao beans into the mortar and start pounding and grinding, adding some heat with your hairdryer as you go. Keep going until a gritty paste is formed. Be patient, as this takes time – and some muscle power. The warmth you apply will allow the cocoa butter in the beans to soften and melt, making it easier to grind.

Once you have a paste that is pretty fluid, scrape it out into a metal bowl and place it over a pan of hot water, then continue with the rest of the beans. If you like, you can grind all the beans in one day and let the cocoa mass set, then melt it the next day, ready for the next stage.

Taste the 100 per cent cocoa mass, as you have just released so many complex and intense flavours and aromas. It will be robust and strong at this stage.

Sweetening your cocoa mass

Let's make 70 per cent dark chocolate with the cocoa mass you have created. The ratio is 70 per cent cocoa mass to 30 per cent sugar.

In a bowl, mix together 350g (12oz) of your cocoa mass and 105g (3¼oz) icing sugar. Mix the two together and grind this mixture in the pestle and mortar until a paste is formed. You may need to apply some heat to the mix with a hairdryer or heat gun to gently help release the cocoa butter. Keep mixing and grinding until a mass of brown paste is formed. If it's really thick, you can add some melted cocoa butter, which can be bought online, but do make sure it's pure, and for food use rather than cosmetic use.

Transfer to a bowl: this is your 70 per cent cocoa solids sweetened chocolate. Check the temperature of the chocolate with your digital thermometer. You want it to read 50°C (122°F). If not, you can apply heat with the hairdryer/heat gun once more.

Tempering

Tempering is the recrystallisation process, which makes the chocolate shiny and smooth, and allows it to shrink so it releases from a mould easily. It's worth noting that your chocolate won't be silky smooth, even when tempered, because of the process we've used. It will, however, be amazing, shiny and intoxicating – and you made it from scratch. Wow.

To temper the chocolate, you'll need to be bold and confident. We'll be using the tabletop method, so you'll need a granite or marble surface to work on.

You'll need a palette knife and scraper, just like the ones used to scrape wallpaper off walls.

Pour two thirds of your melted chocolate on to worktop and spread it out to increase the surface area.

Scrape it back into a contained pool of chocolate and repeat until the chocolate just begins to thicken – this will be when it reaches 27°C (80°F). Immediately scrape the chocolate back into the bowl with the remaining one third melted chocolate and mix until all the chocolate is evenly mixed.

The temperature of the chocolate should now be 30–31°C (86–87°F).

Dip the palette knife into the chocolate and allow the chocolate on the knife to set fully. If your chocolate is tempered, it will set evenly and smoothly, without any graininess or swirling on the surface.

At this stage, you can use your tempered chocolate in one of the many recipes in this book, or turn it into your own chocolate bar. If you have a chocolate bar mould, then pour in your tempered chocolate and scrape off any excess. Tap the mould firmly a few times on the worktop to release any air bubbles, then refrigerate for 20 minutes.

If you do not have a chocolate bar mould, then pour your tempered chocolate on to a tray lined with baking paper in large chocolate-button shapes, then refrigerate for 20 minutes maximum.

Once set, turn the mould upside down and tap gently to release what should be a shiny bar of chocolate.

(If your bar has not released from the mould, then your chocolate was not tempered, and it may be stuck in there, unfortunately. You can place the mould in a low oven – 50°C/30°C fan/122°F/gas less than ¼ – for about 10 minutes until the chocolate melts, then use a silicone spatula to scrape out the chocolate and start again. The mould will need to be washed, dried and polished before you use it again.)

Congratulations on making your very first bean-to-bar chocolate bar. Taste it, share it, be proud of it. All your hard work has been worth it.

If you find you have caught the chocolate-making bug, then you can buy cacao melangeurs that do all the hard work for you. They sit on the worktop and can run for up to 72 hours, refining your cacao beans and sugar into super-smooth chocolate. They have changed how so many of us make chocolate and experiment with chocolate recipes. They can also be used for grinding caramelised nuts into praline paste.

Did you know?
To make 1kg (2lb 4oz) chocolate, you need to start with approximately 1.3kg (3lb) beans, as the winnowing and nibbing process reduces your yield.

Recipes for your own chocolate

What can you make with your handmade chocolate? Here are some of my all-time favourite recipes that I wanted to share with you. They are all very easy to make, and use smaller quantities, as you won't be able to make huge batches of chocolate. So really take time to enjoy every bite and taste all the complexities of your own chocolate. These treats are all very special and they will make you feel so much joy.

'Add more joy' chocolate cubes

This isn't really a recipe, but a way to bring joy to the food you enjoy every day. Make your homemade chocolate following the instructions on pages 59–63, but this time, instead of pouring it into a mould, pour it into an ice-cube tray. Refrigerate for 20 minutes, and you will have chunks of chocolate, ready to use whenever you need them. You can keep them in the tray, but don't store them in the fridge: put them somewhere cool and dark, away from strong odours.

Here are a few ideas for how to use your chocolate cubes:

- Next time you make a roast, grate half a chunk into your gravy. It will make it really rich and smooth, and give a wonderful colour.
- Anything you make with minced beef or lamb will come to life with a generous grating of your own chocolate stirred through just before serving, or mixed through your mince before you assemble a lasagne, moussaka or shepherd's pie.
- Grating a small square of chocolate over grilled steak with black pepper adds a subtle sweetness and warmth to the flavour.
- Any dessert can enjoy a grating of your own chocolate, whether it's to decorate the plate or to add flavour. Be generous.
- Add a whole cube to your flat white or latte and stir well to create an amazing mocha.
- Best of all, grate lots into a bacon or grilled halloumi sandwich. Try it, it's amazing.

The opportunities are endless, so choose a dinner table–worthy plate or slate, add a small grater or peeler and place on the dinner table with a chunk of chocolate so that everyone can find their way of adding more joy to their food.

Caramel chocolate pot

Yes: more indulgence! This is truly sweet and decadent. Not much more to say, really, other than make it, love it, enjoy it, share it – and make it again.

Melt the butter, salt and sugar together in a saucepan over a medium heat. Once the mixture starts bubbling, remove from the heat.

Add the cream, mixing well, then add your chocolate and stir to combine until the chocolate has melted.

Pour into dessert pots, small bowls or coffee cups and allow to set. When cold, refrigerate for 30 minutes before serving.

∾∾ **To add more joy** Caramel can be flavoured with almost anything, so add spices, coffee, herbs, alcohol or orange zest.

Makes 2 pots

75g (2¾oz) unsalted butter
½ teaspoon crushed sea salt flakes
75g (2¾oz) unrefined light muscovado sugar
75ml (2¾fl oz) double cream
100g (3½oz) your homemade chocolate (page 59)

Chocolate sauce

When was the last time you said, 'That was the best chocolate sauce I've ever had on my ice cream?' Yes, I know. It's almost always from a squeezy bottle, and it's probably never even been near any real chocolate. Even in high-end gelato shops, I see cheap chocolate syrups being used – why would you ruin your amazing gelato with these awful flavoured syrups? No more! This recipe is so easy – and you'll have the added satisfaction of knowing that it's your chocolate making your ice-cream sundaes taste so wonderful.

Combine the water and syrup in a saucepan over a medium heat and bring to a simmer.

Melt your chocolate in a heatproof bowl set over a pan of hot water, then pour in the hot syrup and water. Whisk well to combine, then add the vanilla extract and whisk again.

Serve warm over ice cream, cakes or fresh berries.

∾∾ **To add more joy** Add the grated zest of 1 orange for a luscious dark chocolate–orange sauce, use espresso instead of water for a coffee–chocolate sauce, or add a glug of your favourite spirit for a super–boozy sauce.

Makes 350ml (12fl oz)

150ml (5fl oz) water
50g (1¾oz) golden syrup, runny honey or agave syrup
200g (7oz) your homemade chocolate (page 59)
1 teaspoon vanilla extract

Sugar and spice cocoa nib kisses

I love texture in chocolate, especially crunch, so these are a winner every time and perfect if you fancy a mix of crunch, melt and spice. The spices here are the ones I love best, but they're just a guide, so if you don't like cinnamon but love ginger, simply make a swap. The same goes for any of the spices.

Line a baking tray with baking paper.

Melt half of your homemade chocolate in a heatproof bowl set over a pan of hot water, and chop the rest into small pieces. Mix the chopped chocolate into the melted chocolate until everything has melted.

Stir in the rest of the ingredients, then use a teaspoon to dollop small portions on to the prepared baking tray — each one should be about 25g (1oz).

Tap the tray once on the worktop so that each portion becomes slightly spread out, but not too much — it's a kiss, not a button. Refrigerate for 15 minutes to set, then store at room temperature. Present in chocolate boxes as a gift or store in an airtight container for up to 3 months.

To add more joy While your buttons are still unset, add your favourite decorations, glitters or sprinkles.

Makes 25 kisses

200g (7oz) your homemade chocolate (page 59)
100g (3½oz) roasted cocoa nibs
50g (1¾oz) demerara sugar
1 teaspoon ground cinnamon
1 teaspoon grated nutmeg
½ teaspoon black pepper

After-dinner crunchy mint wafers

I love, love, LOVE an after-dinner mint, and I mean any kind: the fondant-filled ones, the peppermint creams and the crunchy ones full of sugary crystals. So I had to include a recipe. Chocolate after dinner is such a joyous experience, as we tend to savour it as part of a special evening: and yes, it's a bit kitsch, but we all love a bit of kitsch, even if we won't admit it.

Line a baking tray with baking paper.

Melt half of your homemade chocolate in a heatproof bowl set over a pan of hot water, and chop the rest into small pieces. Mix the chopped chocolate into the melted chocolate until everything has melted.

Add the sugar and peppermint oil, tasting to check you are happy with the minty–ness.

Pour the chocolate on to the lined tray and spread out to a thickness of 3mm (⅛in). Allow to nearly set.

When the chocolate is just a breath away from being crisp, use a sharp knife or pizza cutter to cut into squares or triangles, leaving them in place on the lined tray. Refrigerate for 15 minutes.

Peel the baking paper off the chocolate and stack the wafers neatly together, ready for post-dinner nibbles. Store in an airtight container in a cool, dry place for up to 6 months.

To add more joy Edible essential oils are vital for adding natural flavours to chocolate, so experiment with other botanicals that complement mint, for example lemon, lemon balm and pine. Don't use essences and flavourings, though, as these are water–based and will not blend with your chocolate.

Makes 20–30 wafers

200g (7oz) your homemade
  chocolate (page 59)
50g (1¾oz) demerara sugar
5–6 drops peppermint oil,
  to taste

Chocolate-coated coffee beans

Coffee and chocolate have been a popular combination for decades, but sadly coffee-flavoured chocolates have fallen out of favour with many of us because so few exist that actually taste anything like real coffee beans. Secretly, I still love those artificial-tasting ones for their nostalgia factor, but when you want real coffee and chocolate, there is only one route to take, and that's the whole coffee bean enrobed in chocolate. It's easy and fast, you get lots of finished product from a small amount of coffee beans, and when you think of how many varieties of coffee and chocolate there are, you begin to realise how many different versions you can make.

Preheat the oven to its lowest temperature and line a baking tray with baking paper.

Melt half of your homemade chocolate in a heatproof bowl set over a pan of hot water, and chop the rest into small pieces. Mix the chopped chocolate into the melted chocolate until everything has melted.

Spread out the coffee beans on a baking tray and warm them very gently in the low oven for 2 minutes.

Tip the beans into a large mixing bowl and add half the melted chocolate. Use your hands to mix it all around and coat all the beans in chocolate.

Lift them out on to the lined tray and quickly separate the beans from each other so they don't all stick together. Allow them to set for 2 minutes.

Return the beans to the bowl and add the remaining chocolate. Repeat the coating process above. Once the chocolate–covered beans are on the lined tray and separated, leave them to set for 15 minutes.

They are now ready to eat, bag or jar up, or give as gifts. They will keep in a jar in a cool, dry place for up to 6 months.

To add more joy Once your beans are coated and set, scatter over edible gold shimmer powder and mix well to create golden coffee beans. They look incredible and will impress anyone you offer them to or give to as a gift.

Makes 100g (3½oz)

100g (3½oz) roasted coffee beans
200g (7oz) your homemade chocolate (page 59)

The best chocolate crispy cakes ever

No chocolate book is complete without a chocolate crispy cake recipe, even though the ingredients rarely change. Some additions – chopped nuts, fudge or cookies – can make them the very best (and most sophisticated) crispy cakes ever.

Cut out large squares of baking paper and crumple up really well. Line six teacups or small bowls with the crumpled paper.
Melt your chocolate in a heatproof bowl set over a pan of hot water, then take off the heat and mix in the remaining ingredients until very well combined.

Divide the mixture between the lined cups or bowls. Refrigerate for 20 minutes to set, then remove from the fridge. These will keep in an airtight container in a cool, dry place for up to 1 week.

Makes 6 generous crispy cakes

150g (5oz) your homemade chocolate (page 59)
60g (2oz) crisped rice
40g (1½oz) cocoa nibs
pinch of sea salt

Warm ganache for dipping

There is something so luxurious about dipping something into melted chocolate, whether it's your finger, cookies or fresh fruit. But there is something even more luxurious to dip into, and that's a soft, warm ganache of intense dark chocolate. Experiment by adding a glug of your favourite spirit or liqueur, or a touch of chilli.

Melt your chocolate in a heatproof bowl set over a pan of hot water. In a separate saucepan, bring the cream to a simmer over a medium heat and stir in the salt.

Pour the cream over the melted chocolate and whisk until glossy.

Spoon the glossy ganache into a beautiful bowl and prepare some dipping treats. I like dipping biscotti and brownies in mine.

Makes 1 sharing ganache

200g (7oz) your homemade chocolate (page 59)
100ml (3½fl oz) double cream
pinch of sea salt

Chocolate brittle

Brittle is everything I love about chocolate. You can put anything in it, as a long as it's not wet (so fresh berries are a no-no, but dried fruits are OK). It snaps easily, it's great to share, and it melts really quickly in your mouth, so the flavours are released rapidly.

Line a 20cm (8in) square baking tray with baking paper. Melt your chocolate in a heatproof bowl set over a pan of hot water.

Add the coffee and sea salt to your bowl of melted chocolate and stir to combine.

Pour the chocolate on to the lined tray and spread it out into an even layer. Immediately sprinkle over the almonds and amaretti biscuits, pressing them in if needed.

Refrigerate for 20 minutes, then snap into shards. The brittle will keep in an airtight container in a cool, dry place for up to 3 months.

Makes 1 tray of brittle

200g (7oz) your homemade chocolate (page 59)
7g roasted coffee beans, well crushed or ground
2g crushed sea salt flakes
25g (1oz) toasted almonds, chopped
15g (½oz) crushed amaretti biscuits

Water ganache truffles

A chocolate truffle can only taste as good as the chocolate it's made with. Here, we are using water rather than cream, so that the purity of your homemade chocolate shines like the brightest beacon.

Melt your chocolate in a heatproof bowl set over a pan of hot water. Combine the sugar and water in a saucepan over a high heat and bring to the boil.

Pour this mixture over your melted chocolate and use a hand blender to emulsify.

Allow the ganache to cool, then refrigerate for 1 hour.

Once set, scoop out even-sized balls of ganache. Dust the cocoa powder over a plate and roll the ganache balls through it to coat.

These will keep for up to 2 weeks in the fridge in an airtight container, but let them come up to room temperature before eating.

Makes 30 truffles

200g (7oz) your homemade chocolate (page 59)
50g (1¾oz) unrefined light muscovado sugar
100ml (3½fl oz) water
100g (3½oz) cocoa powder

Branding, advertising and packaging

I felt intense joy when, in 1996, I moved from Yorkshire to London to fulfil my ambition of becoming a pastry chef. To make this even more exciting, I was working for Marco Pierre White at the Criterion Brasserie. I really did have stars in my eyes, and could hardly believe that I had a job in the most beautiful restaurant in London, with a team that was so passionate about cooking. At first, I actually underestimated just *how* passionate they were, and how intensely passionate I too would become about creating only the very best plates of food for seriously foody people.

It was the very first time I had worked with chefs from other countries and different backgrounds, yet we all had one thing in common: our love for chocolate and the chocolate bars of our own childhoods. Names of bars I'd never heard of were flung around: Cadbury Cherry Ripe, an Australian institution that is a blend of cherry and coconut, similar to a Bounty but with a fruity edge; Reese's Peanut Butter Cups, which simply sounded so American I wanted to head to the US immediately just to buy some; and chocolate-coated salted liquorice from Sweden, which sounded so experimental and unusual, and which I have since fallen in love with. I've tried them all over the years, and enjoyed each one (apart from some seriously salty liquorice that dried out my lips so much they cracked). No matter where you are from, you will have a favourite chocolate bar, with a nostalgic story, memory and experience attached to it. It says a lot about how we choose which chocolate bar to eat, and the role advertising and branding play in our choices. In general, I would say I'm not easily led simply by how a wrapper looks or whether I like the font and colours. I want to know what's inside, and what it's going to taste like. Having said that, though, the wrapper, name, colours and message must still draw me in, entice me, tease me and say *EAT ME!*

Classic adverts

I often have fun conversations with friends and colleagues about our favourite chocolate adverts from years gone by. The TV adverts for Cadbury Flake often feature in these reminiscences. The most famous featured a beautiful woman reclining in an extravagantly situated overflowing bath, a Cadbury Flake in hand, with the focus on how she was eating it as she drifted off to a place of no cares, no worries, only enjoyment and fulfilment. I always read this as meaning that eating a Cadbury Flake was going to be better than sex – and who was I to argue? I was only 12 or 13 years old at the time. I was honestly more concerned about the damage the overflowing bath would do to the floor, but that says more about me than the chocolate. I do love a Cadbury Flake, but it's a very messy chocolate bar to eat, so it's not my favourite. Still, this was hugely successful advertising: taking a chocolate bar that could be eaten anywhere into a place where food isn't usually consumed gave the message that the Cadbury Flake was all about taking time for you and removing yourself from the stresses of everyday life. And, of course, it was sexy. In the 1970s, one of the adverts was actually taken off our screens having been deemed too racy, and the iconic strapline associated with these ads, 'Only the crumbliest, flakiest chocolate' was dropped in 2010. Nostalgia kicks in when we lose these iconic adverts and straplines, and we reminisce about the good old days and how great the Cadbury Flake was, even though it hasn't actually gone anywhere.

Another iconic moment for chocolate advertising was in 2007, when Cadbury released an advert for Dairy Milk featuring a gorilla playing drums to the Phil Collins 1981 hit 'In the Air Tonight'. I'm going to be very honest, I didn't like the advert at all. It just didn't speak to me in any way, and definitely didn't make me feel good, which is the intention of most advertising. It's all very subjective, of course, but

A TV advertisement for Cadbury Flake from the 1990s. Chocolate seduction at its very best, how can you resist?

BRANDING, ADVERTISING AND PACKAGING

even though I didn't personally like it, it did stay with me as the cleverest chocolate advert of all time, in my view. There were no images of chocolate melting or pouring; no sexy imagery; nothing at all to actually say it was about chocolate. It was just a man in a gorilla costume, a drum kit and the soundtrack. It went viral, increased sales by 10 per cent and is still a popular go-to on YouTube. So I may not have liked it, but it worked: it's an advert none of us can forget.

We now see fewer adverts for chocolate on TV, as we are encouraged to eat fewer high-fat and high-sugar products, but I'm so grateful that we can still dig into the past via the fantastic invention of the internet to view some of the most fantastical chocolate marketing and advertising imaginable – and none is better than the Cadbury adverts for Milk Tray, which, for four decades from 1968, had us glued to our screens in the gaps between TV shows to see the drama unfold.

Picture it: the dramatic scene of towering cliff tops; the dark figure of a handsome man spots a glamorous yacht and dives from the cliff into the sea; a shark gets perilously close to biting off his leg, but the handsome stranger climbs on to the yacht – all so he can leave a box of Cadbury Milk Tray and his calling card which has no name, just a silhouette of himself. And the strapline was: 'All because the lady loves Milk Tray'. It was very dramatic, with music to match, and very provocative too. I remember feeling that they were like mini *Bond* movies, and wondering if the glamorous lady ever got to meet her mystery stranger. We will never know, but one thing is clear: this was a very successful campaign spanning four decades, with four stunt

An advert for Cadbury Milk Tray from 1956. The advert has the same glamour and romance as the later Bond-style TV advertisements.

Make the day with Cadburys Milk Tray*

*So thickly covered with Cadburys Dairy Milk Chocolate

actors playing the mysterious Milk Tray man, and millions of boxes of Cadbury Milk Tray sold as we fell in love with the drama of the advert and the taste of the chocolates. Which was your favourite chocolate in a Cadbury Milk Tray? Mine was either the Orange Cream or the Hazelnut Whirl. Do I still enjoy a box of Cadbury Milk Tray today? Sadly not as much. Have they changed? Have I changed? Probably both – but I do have very fond memories of removing the cellophane and opening the box, breathing in the plume of intoxicating aromas of chocolate and all the fillings, and the joy of reading the card with all the names, flavours and shapes of the chocolates inside.

We do still see chocolate adverts on our TVs, of course, but they tend to be for the more luxurious or aspirational brands, like Lindt and Ferrero Rocher®.

These adverts all set a scene or create a scenario, planting in our subconscious the seed of when to buy this chocolate, and for what kind of occasion. Think about the Ferrero Rocher® adverts, where a lavish party is being held by 'the ambassador' and a tray of gold-wrapped chocolates arrives stacked high to 'spoil' the guests, to make them feel special. I still truly love a Ferrero Rocher®, but I now prefer to make my own version at home (see page 100). It may not be a lavish embassy party when I choose to bring them out – it's likely to be a movie night with family or friends – but we will enjoy them and feel special all the same. This is the secret to amazing marketing, branding and packaging: it's the full package and it delivers every single time. It's not easy to get this balance just right, but when it is right, we all become loyal customers and make these products part of family tradition.

The Lindt advert for their LINDOR chocolate range gives us the message that this is real chocolate, using all the right language and imagery to seduce you with their passion and vision. We see a chocolatier in the Lindt development kitchen, and WOW – this is the chocolate kitchen of all chocolate kitchens. It's super-luxe, shiny and definitely new. Every time I see this kitchen, I do roll my eyes as I'm sure it doesn't really exist and is just a set to make us part of the fantasy. I know I shouldn't overthink it, but none of my kitchens look that elaborate – or that clean of chocolate. Back to my point: it's an advert that draws us in. It's dreamy and silky-smooth: a very stylish whisk with gorgeous ganache enrobing its wires is lifted from a bowl by the chocolatier, and then a very sensually lipped woman bites into the chocolate, just to show us how good they are and how great they will make us feel. By this time, of course we are all in: we are putting on our shoes to go out to the shop, or placing an online order for same-day delivery. It's 30 seconds packed with positive messaging and promising a luxurious and otherworldly experience. It has everything, right? All the ingredients for a successful chocolate advert.

Wherever you are in the world, chocolate advertising has the most wonderful ability to be luxurious, comforting, magical and fantastical, whether in print or on screen. We want to be taken to that magical place, the place that promises to soothe our stress, feed our souls and make us oooh and ahhh at the TV or social media screen – and all in just 30 seconds. But the adverts are only part of the story of how we fall in love with chocolate. We need to love the brand, the marketing, the packaging and the taste.

Packaging

I am obsessed with chocolate packaging. I know of no other food packaging that is so striking, whether it's fine chocolate or confectionery bars. All over the world, they are so iconic and instantly recognisable: they need to be, as we rely on the design and colours to identify our favourite chocolate bars at a glance. Chocolate has a personality and evokes an emotional reaction – and that's before you have opened it, tasted and fallen in love. So what makes for successful chocolate packaging?

Two of the most famous and recognisable brands worldwide are Cadbury and Hershey. Both companies showcase an astonishing number of products under their brands, and some are global superstars. Cadbury Dairy Milk and Hershey's Kisses are both iconic products and brands in their own right due to their popularity and longevity. Why? It's all down to memorable branding and brand messaging.

Hershey's Kisses were first made in 1907: small, flat-bottomed tear-drop shaped milk chocolates, each hand-wrapped in a strip of silver foil with a paper plume or flag so it could easily be identified against other brands. Their slogan is literally a sweet one that stole the hearts of America at the time they launched: 'A kiss for you'. It was such clever marketing and messaging, as it spoke to everyone in a universal way that was easy to understand and could fit every occasion. With over 70 million Kisses being made every day, including seasonal varieties, they have certainly become iconic in America and around the world. The Hershey's branding is, in my view, very subdued, with blocky letters in silver or brown and the image of a Hershey's Kiss. I know it well and recognise it wherever I go, but I didn't grow up with it and it therefore doesn't pull on my heartstrings in the same way as Cadbury Dairy Milk.

Of course, we all tend to prefer the chocolate we grew up with as children – and for me, that's Cadbury Dairy Milk. I get a warm feeling whenever I see the Cadbury logo. Its regal purple and swirly font, which is the signature of William Cadbury, was adopted in the 1970s, and I think it has the movement of chocolate when it's melted. As a child, I remember the special selling point of the chocolate being that it contained 'A glass and a half of whole milk'. Milk was good for you, and to have a glass and a half in every bar clearly added something special: before even tasting it, you knew it would be super-creamy and milky. This way of advertising chocolate is no longer current, as suggesting that chocolate is a healthy option is incorrect. Cadbury no longer use the phrase in their advertising, but 'a glass and a half' is still part of the Dairy Milk messaging in image form, appearing on the front of all their packaging.

Another world-famous chocolate bar that used a similar advertising method was Mars®, with the hook: 'A Mars a day helps you work, rest and play'. I'm not saying that it misled anyone, as eating a Mars® bar certainly does give you a huge boost of energy from sugar, but that boost will be short and sharp, and then you might have a sugar crash that

Did you know?

The chocolate used in our most common and well-known confectionery bars was technically called 'vegelate' until the year 2000, due to its high percentage of vegetable fats and low quantities of cocoa butter. The European Union compromised, and now allows it to be called chocolate with up to 5 per cent vegetable fats added.

leaves you feeling tired and groggy. With time, education and scientific evidence, the message that sold millions of bars was dropped by Mars®. When it was launched in 1932, the ingredients used in Mars® bars, and in so many chocolate bars, were believed to be good for you – back then, we didn't know how sugar and fat affected our bodies when consumed regularly. Now, we all know everything in moderation is good and OK, so enjoy your Mars® bar without the guilt.

Celebrating the greats

Celebrating some of the all-time greats of the chocolate and confectionery industry means not just tasting them, but also making chocolates inspired by them yourself at home. Some of them are quite technical and tricky to perfect, but we are not looking for perfection – we just want to recreate the joy of these bars in a home environment.

I used social media to ask people the names of their favourite chocolate bars, past and present. These are the top ten answers:

1. Bounty
2. Snickers®
3. Milky Way®
4. Cadbury Bournville Old Jamaica
5. Cadbury Cherry Ripe
6. Cadbury Curly Wurly
7. Cadbury Fuse
8. Ferrero Rocher®
9. Cadbury Creme Egg
10. Twix®

Coconut paradise bar

When I was a child, this type of chocolate always made me feel very special and quite grown-up. Small coconut bars enrobed in thick milk or dark chocolate: what could be more exotic? I loved them, and still do. I particularly like to make them on special occasions (and by that, I mean whenever I fancy one, as they are so easy to make).

To make the filling

Line a baking tray with baking paper.

Gently warm the glucose syrup in a small saucepan over a low heat for 2–3 minutes, then take off the heat and pour into a bowl, along with the coconut, icing sugar and vanilla extract. Mix together to form a mouldable paste. It will very sticky, so you may need to get your hands in to mix and knead it well.

Weigh out 25g (1oz) balls of the sticky coconut mix and shape into small fingers.

Using a palette knife, flatten the top of each finger, then turn over and repeat on the bottom before placing on the prepared baking tray.

To temper the chocolate

Now prepare your chocolate for tempering.

Melt two thirds of your chocolate in a glass or metal bowl over a pan of hot water until it's fully melted. The temperature of the chocolate must not exceed 50°C (122°F).

Remove the bowl from the heat and mix well, then add the remaining chocolate and mix again until all the chocolate has fully melted and the temperature reads 29–30°C (84–86°F).

Recipe continues overleaf

Makes 16 mini bars

100g (3½oz) glucose syrup
150g (5oz) desiccated coconut
75g (2¾oz) icing sugar
1 teaspoon vanilla extract

For enrobing the bars

500g (1lb 2oz) dark or milk
   chocolate

Test that your chocolate is tempered by dipping your palette knife into the chocolate and allowing a little chocolate to set on the blade. If it looks smooth and glossy, not grainy or streaky, then you have tempered your chocolate well.

To enrobe

Brush the top of each of the coconut fingers with two layers of chocolate and leave to set. This will be the base of your bar.

Once the chocolate has set, place the bars on a wire rack with the chocolate on the bottom. Now spoon the tempered chocolate over each bar to fully enrobe and tap the wire rack on the surface so that any excess chocolate drips down.

Use the back of a spoon or fork to create ripples on the surface of the bars, then carefully place them on a fresh tray or plate lined with baking paper. Refrigerate for 10 minutes to set.

You now have 16 beautiful homemade coconut bars that will taste stunning, with a soft middle and a crisp shell. Keep them in a cool, dry place away from heat, sunlight and strong odours. They will keep for up to 3 months, but really they're so delicious, they won't last 3 days.

Did you know?
Britain consumes around 660,900 tonnes (728,518 tons) of chocolate a year, an average of three bars per person a week.

Cosmic bar

This light and fluffy bar evokes more childhood memories for me. The whipped nougat filling within is delicious, and light enough that you could even eat two or three bars! Once you've mastered the nougat method, you'll find it a natural progression to move on to the Peanut Caramel Bar (page 90), which you should find super-easy, because it uses the same whipped nougat filling.

To make the filling

Make the whipped nougat filling according to the instructions on page 91.

To enrobe

Line a baking tray with baking paper.

Lift the filling out of its baking tray and spread a thin layer of tempered chocolate across the top. Allow the chocolate to just about set, then mark out lines for cutting into 16 bars. Refrigerate for 15 minutes, then cut to create 16 individual bars.

Turn the bars over so that the chocolate top becomes the base of the bar. Now dip each bar into the tempered milk chocolate using a dipping fork or table fork, tapping off any excess chocolate, then place on the prepared baking tray.

Create a textured finish on each bar with your fork, then refrigerate for 15 minutes until set.

Share, eat and love the joy of making your own chocolate bars.

Makes 16 bars

For the whipped nougat filling
vegetable oil, for oiling
400g (14oz) unrefined golden
  caster sugar
225g (8oz) glucose syrup
165ml (5½fl oz) water
55g (2oz) dark chocolate
  (60 per cent cocoa solids),
  finely chopped
2 large egg whites
¼ teaspoon sea salt

For enrobing the bars
600g (1lb 5oz) milk chocolate,
  tempered according to the
  instructions on pages 63 or 84

Caribbean rum and raisin

I remember my great-grandad loving this kind of chocolate, and my mum still loves it today. It's a sweet but dark chocolate, flavoured with rum, with whole raisins running through the chocolate – so nothing too complex, but it is hard to replicate, as anything wet cannot be put directly into the chocolate, so adding a glug of rum just won't work. Commercially, a rum flavouring would be used in the bar, but I wanted to keep this pure and natural, so only real rum will do. Therefore, I've opted for rum-soaked raisins. This way, every time you sink your teeth into the bar, each raisin will release a gush of real rum.

Place the raisins in a container with a lid and pour over the rum. Seal the lid and leave for 5 days. This gives the raisins time to soak up lots of rum.

When you're ready to make the bars, temper your chocolate according to the instructions on pages 63 or 84.

Lift the raisins out of the rum and dry them using a clean towel or paper towels.

Stir them into the chocolate, then pour into bar moulds, or if you don't have bar moulds, then dollop discs of the chocolate and raisins on to a tray lined with baking paper and leave for 15–20 minutes to set. Store in an airtight container in a cool, dry place for 2 months.

Makes 2 × 100g (3½oz) bars or 4 × 50g (1¾oz) discs

100g (3½oz) raisins
100ml (3½fl oz) dark rum
350g (12oz) low-percentage dark chocolate (55–60 per cent cocoa solids)

Peanut caramel bar

These are a favourite of mine, as I love the combination of toasted peanuts and caramel that sits in a thick layer above a soft whipped nougat, all enrobed in thick milk chocolate. These are super-sweet and indulgent, and you are not going to want to share, so make lots – and then lots more.

To make the whipped nougat filling

Line a 20cm (8in) square baking tray with baking paper and oil the paper well with vegetable oil.

Place the sugar, glucose syrup and water in a medium saucepan over a medium heat and stir until the sugar dissolves, brushing down the sides of the saucepan with a wet pastry brush to prevent sugar crystals from forming. Simmer, without stirring, until the temperature on a digital or sugar thermometer reaches 125–126°C (257–259°F), then remove from the heat.

Meanwhile, melt the chocolate in a heatproof bowl set over a pan of hot water. Don't let the water boil, or it can burn the chocolate.

Place the egg whites in a stand mixer fitted with the whisk attachment and whisk on high speed until soft peaks form.

With the mixer still on high speed, slowly add the sugar syrup, pouring it in down the side of the bowl. Continue to whisk until very glossy and stiff.

Remove from the mixer and fold in the melted chocolate until smooth. Scrape the mixture into the prepared tin and smooth the surface by oiling your hands and gently pressing it down. Leave to cool for 2 hours.

Recipe continues overleaf

Makes 16 bars

For the whipped nougat filling
vegetable oil, for oiling
400g (14oz) unrefined golden
    caster sugar
225g (8oz) glucose syrup
165ml (5½fl oz) water
55g (2oz) dark chocolate
    (60 per cent cocoa solids),
    finely chopped
2 large egg whites
¼ teaspoon sea salt

For the peanut caramel
150g (5oz) shelled peanuts
360ml (12fl oz) sweetened
    condensed milk
90g (3¼oz) unsalted butter
370g (13oz) demerara sugar
1 teaspoon sea salt flakes,
    well crushed
1 teaspoon vanilla extract

For enrobing the bars
800g (1lb 12oz) milk chocolate,
    tempered according to the
    instructions on pages 63 or 84

To make the peanut caramel

Preheat the oven to 175°C/155°C fan/345°F/gas 3½.

Place the peanuts on a baking tray and roast for 15 minutes, then set aside to cool.

Meanwhile, place all of the remaining peanut caramel ingredients in a saucepan over a low heat. Simmer, stirring all the time, for 10–12 minutes until the caramel turns a light golden colour.

Scatter the peanuts over the cooled nougat slab, then pour the caramel evenly over the top, ensuring all the peanuts are covered. Leave for 2 hours to set.

Once cold and set, lift out of the tin and place upside down on a piece of baking paper, so the peanut caramel layer is now on the bottom.

To enrobe

Line a second tray with baking paper.

Spread a thin layer of tempered chocolate over the whipped nougat (this will be the bottom of the bars). Just before it sets, mark 16 bars in the chocolate.

Refrigerate for 15 minutes then cut through to create 16 individual bars.

Turn the bars over so that the peanut caramel layer is on top. Now dip each bar into the tempered milk chocolate to fully enrobe, then place on the prepared baking tray. Create a textured finish on each bar with your fork, then place in the fridge for 15 minutes to set before removing. These will keep in an airtight container in a cool, dry place for up to 6 months.

Did you know?
Mole, the savoury sauce from Mexico, often contains a small amount of chocolate for extra richness.

Chocolate and caramel shortbread fingers

Making and working with caramel can be intimidating at first, so take your time and don't rush this process.

To make the shortbread and caramel layers

Preheat the oven to 180°C/160°C fan/350°F/gas 4 and line a 20cm (8in) square baking tray with baking paper.

Mix together all the shortbread ingredients and press them into the prepared tray with the back of a metal spoon, trying to spread out the mixture in as even a layer as possible. Bake for 10 minutes.

While the shortbread is baking, place all of the caramel ingredients in a saucepan over a low heat. Simmer, stirring all the time, for 10 minutes until the caramel turns a light golden colour.

Remove the shortbread from the oven and pour the caramel over the top. Return the tray to the oven, then turn the oven off and leave it in there in the residual heat for 12 minutes.

Remove from the oven and leave to cool in the tray on a wire rack for 15 minutes, then carefully lift out of the tray. Trim the edges of the shortbread and caramel slab, then cut into 9 long fingers. Cut these in half to give you 18 fingers. Place on a wire rack until completely cold.

To enrobe

Line a clean baking tray with baking paper.

Brush the bottom of each finger with the tempered milk chocolate and allow to set in the fridge for 5 minutes.

Turn the fingers over, then, using a dipping fork or table fork, submerge each one in the chocolate, tapping off any excess. Place on the prepared baking tray and use the fork to create a ripple effect on each finger before the chocolate sets. Refrigerate for 15 minutes to set.

Allow the fingers to come to room temperature, then it's soopa-doopa joy time: get the kettle on, and get ready to dunk. These will keep in an airtight container in a cool, dry place for up to 1 month.

Makes 18 fingers

For the shortbread
120g (4oz) unsalted butter, melted
70g (2½oz) unrefined golden caster sugar
180g (6¼oz) plain flour
15g (½oz) cornflour

For the caramel
240ml (8¼fl oz) sweetened condensed milk
60g (2¼oz) unsalted butter
25g (1oz) demerara sugar
½ teaspoon sea salt flakes, well crushed
1 teaspoon vanilla extract

For enrobing the fingers
500g (1lb 2oz) milk chocolate, tempered according to the instructions on pages 63 or 84

Chewy cherry and coconut bar

I first had a cherry and coconut chocolate bar in 1996 when working as pastry chef for Marco Pierre White. These deliciouse bars have a very coconutty filling, with delicate glace cherries, and are enrobed in dark chocolate. Here is my recipe, so you can enjoy them too.

To make the filling

Crush the glace cherries with a fork, then mix all the ingredients together by hand or in a stand mixer with the paddle attachment.

Place the mixture between two sheets of baking paper and roll out to a thickness of 5mm (¼in). Peel off the top piece of paper and leave to rest for an hour.

To enrobe

Line a baking tray with baking paper.

Spread a layer of tempered chocolate over the top of the filling and allow to just set. Cut into 16 rectangles measuring about 14.5 × 2.5cm (5¾ × 1in) and trim off any rough edges.

Now turn each bar over, then dip into the chocolate to fully coat. Tap off any excess chocolate and place on the lined tray.

Refrigerate for 15 minutes, then store in an airtight container in a cool, dry place. Eat within 1 month of making.

Makes 16 mini bars

For the filling

75g (2¾oz) glace cherries
105g (3¾oz) desiccated coconut
50g (1¾oz) condensed milk
50g (1¾oz) glucose syrup
50g (1¾oz) icing sugar
6 drops of natural cherry flavouring

For enrobing the bars

200g (7oz) dark chocolate (60–65 per cent cocoa solids), tempered according to the instructions on pages 63 or 84

Smooshed bar

This bar is a smoosh of milk chocolate, peanuts, raisins, crispy cereal and fudge pieces. So it's not too challenging to make: a bit like a crispy cake, but with lots more going on. Every bite will have crunch and chew, fudge and fruit. It's a wonderful bar to make with kids, as it's so easy and the results are super-delicious.

To make the filling

Preheat the oven to 170°C/150°C fan/340°F/gas 3½ and line a 20cm (8in) square baking tray with baking paper.

Place the peanuts in a small roasting tray and toast in the oven for 10 minutes, then chop into small pieces.

Meanwhile, melt the milk chocolate in a heatproof bowl set over a pan of hot water.

In a bowl, mix together the peanuts, raisins, fudge pieces and puffed rice cereal, then pour in the melted chocolate and mix well. Transfer the crunchy, chocolatey mixture to the prepared baking tray and spread out in an even layer. Place another piece of baking paper on top and press down to flatten.

Refrigerate for 20 minutes, then take out and use a large knife cut the filling into 16 bars. You may need to trim the edges off to perfectly square off the edges. Return to the refrigerator for 20 minutes.

To enrobe

Line a clean tray with baking paper.

Spread some of the tempered chocolate on the bottom of each bar, then allow it to set fully by refrigerating for 5 minutes.

Turn the bars over so the chocolate is on the bottom, then dip each one into the chocolate using a dipping fork or table fork, tapping to remove any excess. Place on the prepared baking tray and use the fork to create ripple marks on top of the bars.

Refrigerate for 15 minutes to set, then it's time to enjoy them, share them and, of course, relish in the achievements of having made this wonderfully textured bar. These will keep in an airtight container in a cool, dry place for up to 3 months.

Makes 16 bars

For the filling

100g (3½oz) peanuts

500g (1lb 2oz) milk chocolate

65g (2¼oz) raisins, roughly chopped

50g (1¾oz) vanilla fudge, chopped into 5mm (¼in) pieces

45g (1½oz) puffed rice cereal

For enrobing the bars

500g (1lb 2oz) milk chocolate, tempered according to the instructions on pages 63 or 84

BRANDING, ADVERTISING AND PACKAGING

Fondant-filled egg

I have one of these every Easter, and that's usually enough for me, as they are so sweet and indulgent. Mine is much bigger than versions you can buy, so brace yourself for a sugar high! You will need four small Easter egg moulds: the ones I use are 7cm (2¼in) high, but feel free to go smaller and adjust the quantities accordingly. Fondant is usually flavoured with vanilla, but you can get creative by adding your own flavourings, like peppermint, orange or lemon oils.

To make the eggshells

Clean your egg moulds with a microfibre cloth to remove any impurities.

Fill each egg cavity with tempered chocolate and tap the mould to release any air bubbles. Invert the mould so any excess chocolate can flow out, then scrape the edges of the mould to clean the edges of the eggs.

Place the moulds on a sheet of baking paper, facedown so any excess chocolate can drip on to the paper. Leave for 5 minutes, then lift the moulds off the paper and refrigerate for 15 minutes.

Check that the egg halves have been released from the moulds by lifting one out. If they have not, refrigerate once more and try again. If they have still not released, then your chocolate is not tempered. Place the moulds in a very low oven (50°C/30°C fan/122°F/gas less than ¼) until the chocolate has melted, then use a silicone spatula to scrape the chocolate out. You will need to temper it again and thoroughly clean and dry the mould.

To make the fondant filling

Meanwhile, make the fondant filling by combining the sugar and water in a small saucepan over a medium heat and bringing to a simmer. Remove from the heat and allow to cool.

In a bowl, combine the sugar syrup with the grated fondant icing until a soft fondant is formed. It should fall from a spoon but not be too runny.

Spoon out 6 heaped teaspoons of the fondant into a small bowl and add the colouring until you have a vibrant yolk colour.

Makes 4 eggs

For the eggshells
500–600g (1lb 2oz–1lb 5oz) milk chocolate, tempered according to the instructions on pages 63 or 84

For the fondant filling
100g (3½oz) unrefined golden caster sugar
100ml (3½fl oz) water
up to 500g (1lb 2oz) shop-bought fondant icing, grated
yellow or orange food colouring paste

For finishing the eggs
25g (1oz) milk chocolate

To construct

Spoon the white fondant into each chocolate egg half, then spoon a little of the yolk fondant into each half.

Melt the milk chocolate for finishing in a small bowl suspended over a pan of hot water. Once melted, allow to cool. Once cool but still fluid, pipe or brush the chocolate around the edges of four of the egg halves.

Carefully lift the other egg halves and stick the eggs together, sealing in the fondant. Leave the eggs to fully set for 20 minutes. Now it's time to indulge and enjoy your larger-than-life fondant-filled eggs.

Wrap them in cellophane or decorative food-safe foil wrappers, and there you have it: Happy Easter (or Happy Anyday)! These eggs will keep in a cool, dry place for up to 3 months.

Tip: Any leftover fondant can be stored in an airtight container or sealed food bag for up to 3 months and used at a later date for more eggs.

Did you know?
The biggest-selling chocolate bar in the world is the Snickers®, which has colossal sales of $3.57 billion at the time of writing. The bar was released in 1942, and was named after the Mars family's favourite horse.

Hazelnut praline bonbons

These are indulgent and very special but they are not easy to make so read through the recipe in full before you begin and don't worry if they don't look perfect!

To make the filling

Preheat the oven to 170°C/150°C fan/340°F/gas 3½.

Scatter the hazelnuts over a baking tray and roast for 10 minutes. Tip the roasted hazelnuts, still hot, into a blender with the vegetable oil and blend, then add the icing sugar and continue blending. When it's as smooth as you can get it, add the cocoa powder, melted chocolate, vanilla extract and salt.

To construct

Cut out 48 pieces of clingfilm, each one 10cm (4in) square, and lay two pieces together, one on top of the other.

Transfer the hazelnut filling to a medium-sized piping bag with a 5mm (¼in) plain nozzle. Pipe a dome of the filling on to the clingfilm, then place a toasted hazelnut on top, pressing it in. Pipe over a little more of the filling to cover. Bring up the corners of the clingfilm and twist the top to form a roughly shaped ball. Repeat to make 24 of these little parcels, then freeze them all for 15 minutes.

Unwrap each ball and roll each one in your hands until evenly round and slightly sticky. Scatter the crushed wafers over a plate and roll the balls through them, then roll again in your hands to push the wafer pieces into the filling. You may need to do this twice. Place all the chocolates in the fridge for 15 minutes.

To enrobe

Line a baking tray with baking paper.

Mix the two chocolates together, then melt and temper (see pages 63 or 84). Once tempered, stir in the chopped nuts.

Using your hands, carefully roll each chocolate ball in the tempered nutty chocolate, then place on the prepared baking tray for 30 minutes to set.

Keep for up to 2 weeks in an airtight container in a cool, dry place.

Makes 24 bonbons

For the chocolate hazelnut filling
225g (8oz) hazelnuts
2 tablespoons vegetable or hazelnut oil
120g (4oz) icing sugar
35g (1¼oz) cocoa powder
45g (1½oz) dark chocolate (60 per cent cocoa solids), melted
1 teaspoon vanilla extract
1 teaspoon sea salt

For the centre
24 roasted hazelnuts

For the wafer shell
50g (1¾oz) shop-bought ice-cream wafers, crushed into very small pieces

For enrobing the bonbons
300g (10½oz) milk chocolate
100g (3½oz) dark chocolate (70 per cent cocoa solids)
100g (3½oz) roasted hazelnuts, finely chopped

To add more joy If you prefer a different nut to hazelnut then try using pecans, almonds or even sunflower seeds if you are nut free. Of course you could use either white or dark chocolate too. For extra glamour, wrap each bonbon in coloured foil.

How to have fun with chocolate

Working with chocolate is so much fun – and very, very messy. However, it can sound incredibly daunting and technically challenging in the beginning. That's why it's important to make sure there is room for having fun.

I started having fun with chocolate at a very young age: it was very simple things, like melted chocolate for decorating, making chocolate crispy cakes or dipping marshmallows into melted chocolate and puffed rice to scoff all in one. This is all very easy stuff and it's how most of us begin our creative and fun time with chocolate. Melted chocolate not only offers you the best way of experiencing its aromas, but it's also a wonderful texture to eat – and to look at. Every time I pour melted chocolate onto a marble surface or into moulds, it's mesmerising and wonderful. So, how can you take melted chocolate and have some fun? How can you mould, sculpt and play with chocolate at home in a way that extends beyond just making cakes, bars and chocolates? This is where we have some fun, make a mess and explore your inner creativity – and no matter how practised you think you are creatively, I promise you will find things in this chapter that fill you with creative joy.

Wrapping a cake

So, you've baked my Chocolate Cake (page 158) and covered it with chocolate buttercream, but it still looks a bit naked. What can you do to make it really pop? Wrapping it in chocolate is the answer. It's like wrapping a car in vinyl to give it a sleek new look. This can be a little fiddly on your first attempt, but it won't take you long to master this wonderful technique.

Measure the circumference of the cake with a piece of string or by measuring the cake tin used to bake the cake in, then cut your acetate or paper so that it's the right size to wrap around the cake.

At this point, you can use the crumpling method (page 108) to make the wrap look incredibly architectural, or you can leave the paper smooth for the super shine of tempered chocolate. Whichever method you choose, lay the paper or acetate on your worktop, then spread the chocolate evenly over the top, using a palette knife to distribute it carefully and evenly. Allow the chocolate to sit for a few minutes until it's half set, so fudgy to the touch and not wet–looking.

Lift the paper or acetate from the top corners and carefully wrap it around the cake, chocolate side facing in, positioning it so the bottom of the sheet is in line with the base of the cake.

Smooth and press the chocolate on to the cake, wrapping it around so that the two ends meet. Refrigerate for 20 minutes.

Now, starting from one corner, carefully peel away the paper or acetate to reveal your masterpiece.

You will need

a baked and iced cake
acetate (sheets or a roll) or baking paper.
800g (1 lb 12oz) dark, milk or white chocolate, tempered according to the instructions on pages 63 or 84

To add more joy The paper or acetate can be decorated. Try piping chocolate in a pattern, or dusting shimmer powders over the paper before spreading the chocolate over the top. Revealing what you have created will always be a surprise and a joy.

Working with tempered chocolate

You must have practised your tempering (see pages 63 and 84) to make the following creations, as your chocolate needs strength to hold its shape and to deliver the stunning shine we all love. So practise lots, be confident and have as much fun as you can.

Balloon bowls

I love balloon bowls: they are simple to make and bring super joy to everyone, from kids at birthday parties to grown-ups at dinner parties. They are edible vessels for holding whatever you like – an ice-cream sundae, fruit salad, chocolate mousse, tiramisu, or even, for very special days, your breakfast cereal.

Line a baking tray with baking paper.

Wash the balloons in warm water and dry them well. Once dry, blow them up, trying to get them all to a similar size. Tie a tight knot in the neck of each balloon.

Have your chocolate in a bowl that the balloon just fits into, so that when you dip the balloon into the chocolate, it comes up the sides of the balloon by at least halfway to two thirds.

Holding the first balloon by the knot, dip it into the chocolate, then shake off any excess chocolate and place on the prepared baking tray to set.

Repeat this process with all the balloons, then, once set, dip them all again so that the chocolate is double layered. Place the dipped balloons in the fridge for 10 minutes to set.

Now comes the fun bit: popping the balloons to reveal your chocolate bowl. I still love this part, especially if I'm making these with children. Carefully pop each balloon and peel away from the chocolate.

You can use the bowls as they are, but just check to see if there are any holes in the base. If there are, patch them up with a little melted chocolate to seal, so that any liquid does not flood through. If you like, you can dip the rim of the bowls in more melted chocolate and then into sprinkles, which really adds colour and joy to the bowls. Keep somewhere cool, but not in the fridge. They can be made in advance and will keep for up to 6 months, but they're very fragile so need to be stored in a container that has enough space to hold them without touching each other.

To add more joy If you like, you can use another type of chocolate for the second layer. If you are feeling even more adventurous, why not have milk, dark and white chocolate in separate bowls and dip the balloon into each a little less each time so that your bowls have a striped effect.

You will need

8–10 small water balloon

500g (1lb 2oz) chocolate, tempered according to the instructions on pages 63 or 84

Crumpled chocolate

I love, love, *love* crumpled chocolate: it has a real WOW factor and looks impossibly difficult to create, yet it's so easy. Once you've tried it, you will use this technique on so many of your cakes and desserts. This is the technique I've used for my Chocolate tart recipe on page 202.

Scrunch up your baking paper or acetate sheet really well, then unroll it but don't smooth it out. You want to keep those angles and some of the crumpled structure.

If you're using shimmer powders or cocoa powder, dust them over the baking paper or acetate. Then apply your chocolate, painting it on to the paper or acetate with a pastry brush.

Refrigerate for 15 minutes, then peel off the paper to reveal your amazing crumpled chocolate. It's now ready to be used whole for real drama, or broken up to use on your dessert.

You can keep crumpled chocolate in an airtight container in a cool, dark place for up to 6 months, perfect for any time you want to pimp up a dessert, hot chocolate or ice-cream sundae.

You will need

baking paper or acetate sheets measuring about 21 × 30cm (8¼ × 11¾in)

150g (5oz) dark, milk or white chocolate per sheet, tempered according to the instructions on pages 63 or 84

To add more joy Dust over some shimmer powders (great on milk and dark chocolate) or cocoa powder (great on white chocolate).

Chocolate modelling paste

Chocolate modelling paste is a fantastic alternative to fondant, and it can be used in pretty much the same way. You can roll it out, mould it, colour it and cover cakes with it – and it tastes of wonderful chocolate.

I've used chocolate modelling paste for at least 20 years, for so many fantastic creations. The most fun and memorable was in 2005, when I created a set of chocolate jewellery for a fashion show and a hat for a day at the races entirely decorated with modelling chocolate.

To use modelling chocolate successfully, you need to practise lots and work quickly, especially when making thin, delicate pieces, as it starts to set rapidly and the surface may crack. Play with it like you did as a child with plasticine and clay, by warming it in your hands and kneading until it's pliable and mouldable.

Dark chocolate modelling paste

Melt the chocolate in a heatproof bowl set over a pan of very hot water. Add the syrup and mix well until you have a smooth paste.

Immediately place in a plastic food bag, then flatten and seal. Allow to cool fully before using.

Makes 375g (13oz) paste

250g (9oz) dark chocolate
(60–70 per cent cocoa solids)
125g (4½oz) golden syrup or
glucose syrup

White chocolate modelling paste

Melt the white chocolate in a heatproof bowl set over a pan of very hot water, stirring until smooth. If you want to use food colouring, stir it in now.

In a small bowl or jug, mix the warm water into the syrup, then pour this mixture into your chocolate and mix well.

Immediately place in a plastic food bag, then flatten and seal. Allow to cool fully before using.

Makes 325g (11½oz) paste

250g (9oz) white chocolate
fat–soluble food colouring
(optional)
1 teaspoon warm water
75g (2¾oz) golden syrup
or glucose syrup

Covering cakes

Modelling chocolate is a great alternative to fondant and it has a beautiful sheen when draped over cakes.

Dust your worktop with cornflour before you begin to prevent the modelling chocolate from sticking. (If you have a pair of tights or stockings that you are going to throw away, give them a wash and dry, then cut off the foot and put some cornflour in it before tying a knot in the top. Then use this to dust on your cornflour.)

Knead the modelling chocolate and roll it out to a thickness of about 5mm (¼in). You'll need to work quickly and in a cool room, as a warm room will cause the chocolate to melt and become too sticky to work with.

Roll the modelling chocolate around your rolling pin and drape it over your buttercream-primed cake. Smooth it over neatly, or allow it to drape over like velvet. Trim off any excess.

Use a clean, soft brush to remove any cornflour. The warmth of your hands as you work will bring back the chocolate's sheen.

You will need

cornflour, for dusting

a 20–25cm (8–10in) baked cake, primed with buttercream

4 batches of dark or white modelling chocolate (see opposite)

Using transfer deco sheets

Transfer sheets are the easiest way to apply vibrant, bespoke and individual designs to chocolate. There are so many designs available, meaning you can create a look for any theme or festivity. Transfer sheets are a plastic sheets that have been printed using coloured cocoa butter. Note that some manufacturers use palm oil and artifical colours, so check carefully.

Bear in mind the type of chocolate you will be using your transfer on. Bright, light colours will really pop against darker chocolate, while darker colours look striking on white chocolate. You must have perfectly tempered chocolate to achieve a flawless finish from a transfer sheet; if your chocolate isn't tempered, then the design may not stick, and you will have a patchy finish. You can either spread tempered chocolate on to a transfer sheet and then cut out the shapes you want while the chocolate is still on the sheet, or cut the sheet into specific shapes before the tempered chocolate is applied.

Some transfer sheets are created to marry with magnetic chocolate moulds, which are available to buy online. These moulds give you incredibly defined angles and lines, with a super-flat surface so that the transfer can be applied with a clean finish. The moulds come in two parts: a metal sheet and a polycarbonate mould, which has magnets set into it. The transfer sheet sits on the metal base, and then the mould attaches on top via the magnets. When the mould is filled with chocolate, the chocolate and the transfer print meet. When the chocolate sets, the design is set into the chocolate.

Shards

I use shards so often I always have a container ready for an impromptu cake or dessert. They simply transform a dull, flat surface into something architecturally stunning, bringing height, shape and texture.

Spread your tempered chocolate over your chosen paper or acetate sheet in a layer around 2–3mm (1/16–1/8in) thick.

Allow the chocolate to just set, then swiftly use a sharp knife to score triangular shards through the chocolate, either randomly or with as much precision as you can. Try not to cut through the baking paper or plastic.

Place a sheet of clean baking paper over the shards, then sit a baking tray on top and leave it there for 30 minutes until the chocolate is fully set.

Lift off the baking tray and refrigerate your shards for 10 minutes.

Peel off the paper or acetate, and your shards are ready for action. They will keep in an airtight container in a cool, dry place for up to 6 months.

To add more joy You can achieve a wavy finish, as shown opposite, by using a piece of flexibile plastic that is bent while the chocolate sets. Dusting a shimmer powder onto the paper or acetate sheet before you apply the chocolate adds a touch of sparkle.

You will need

baking paper, deco transfer sheets or acetate sheets measuring about 21 × 30cm (8¼ × 11¾in)

200g (7oz) dark, milk or white chocolate per sheet, tempered according to the instructions on pages 63 or 84

Chocolate spikes and spirals

For dramatic and striking decoration for a celebration cake or for a plated chocolate dessert, my chocolate spikes and spirals are fantastic. They are very easy to make, and when made with vibrantly coloured white modelling chocolate, they are a fun and easy way to decorate a birthday cake.

Knead your chocolate modelling paste until pliable and roll it into balls in lots of different sizes, depending on how big you want your spikes or spirals to be.

On your worktop, roll the balls of paste one at a time, pressing more on one end to form long spikes. Place on baking paper to set for at least 24 hours.

When they are set, they can be used on your cakes and desserts. Make them in advance and keep in an airtight container somewhere cool for up to 6 months. They are fragile, so take care when handling them.

To make a spiral, follow the method above and then, once you have rolled your long spike, immediately wrap it around an artist's paint brush or wooden spoon handle (or a chopstick if your spike is delicate and small). Slide the spiral off the handle and allow it to set as before.

See page 110 for chocolate modelling paste ingredients and recipe

Did you know?
Chcolate makes an appearance in Mozart's opera *Cosi Fan Tutti*, when a maid is tempted into drinking some she has prepared for her mistress.

Chocolate roses

Chocolate roses and flowers may feel a little old school and kitsch, but vibrant kitsch never really goes out of fashion, and there is always an occasion when a cake or cupcake needs some floral joy. This can be quite fiddly, but, like everything, practice is the secret to creating a lifelike chocolate flower or rose.

Take a piece of chocolate modelling paste about the size of a large grape. Roll it into a ball, then, on a clean worktop, roll it to form a long cone shape.

Flatten one edge of the cone from the thick end to the thin end.

Roll the cone from the narrowest end up to the widest end to form the centre of the rose.

Roll smaller balls of paste for the internal petals and smooth them out one by one, flattening into smooth, paper-thin disc shapes.

Wrap the small petal around the central bud, then add the next, overlapping slightly and using three petals to complete every full rotation of the rose.

Continue, making the balls of paste a little bigger as you go to fit around your rose. When you have a full rose, nip off any excess paste from underneath so it can sit neatly on your cake.

You can apply shimmer powders or airbrush colour, and you could even add green leaves made with coloured white modelling chocolate.

Allow the roses to set overnight and handle with care, as they will be fragile.

See page 110 for chocolate modelling paste ingredients and recipe

Chocolate in popular culture

This is an exciting and fun chapter, looking at where and how chocolate has become part of everyday popular culture across the globe. We'll look at how chocolate is referenced in music, art, film and literature, we'll learn about the famous faces and voices behind some of our favourite chocolate brands, and we'll discover how a bestselling book was transformed into a blockbuster movie whose characters brought fine chocolate into every sitting room and cinema. Superstar singers and performers have referenced chocolate in their material for decades, while artists have taken inspiration from cacao and chocolate for hundreds of years. I'll be looking at some of the most whimsical and wonderful creations, including animals, Lego, shoes, celebrity portraits and furniture made from chocolate, as well as historical art where cacao is revered and precious.

When we look at its unbelievably long history, its seductive powers and the way it makes us happy, it's no wonder that chocolate holds such an important position in so many cultures. It has been respected, revered and valued, from its importance to the Aztec, Olmec and Maya cultures, to its prominent position in the present day. Whoever, or whatever, gave us this unbelievable gift knew how much we would fall in love with it. We see, hear, touch and taste chocolate and cacao every day, in so many forms, from food and fragrance to cosmetics and commercials: it's part of our everyday lives, and we all celebrate it in our own ways, big and small.

So, I'm going to share some of my favourite 'chocolate moments' in popular culture. I know you will have your own, too, so please do share your stories with me on social media, as I am always fascinated to hear about other people's chocolate experiences.

Film

***Willy Wonka and the Chocolate Factory* (1971)** For so many of us, this is the most important chocolate film in moving picture history, based on Roald Dahl's book *Charlie and the Chocolate Factory*, which was first published in 1964. It tells the story of Charlie Bucket, who wins a Golden Ticket to the world's most magical and wonderful

The inventing room of Willy Wonka's Chocolate Factory: where my fascination with chocolate started.

chocolate factory, where he'll meet with Mr Willy Wonka himself. But once he gets there, nothing is quite what it seems: everything is edible and just a little bit fantastical. My memories of watching Willy Wonka in his mesmerising factory were permanently cast in chocolate when I was six years old. It was the Christmas of 1979, and I remember watching Charlie Bucket and Willy Wonka on TV. Every colour in the film was so saturated and intense that I wished the whole world could be that colourful. I am assuming that you have seen this iconic film: if you have not, stop reading right now, grab a bookmark (which I hope is your favourite chocolate bar wrapper), go and watch the film, then come back. If you don't, then I will spoil it for you, so go on ... I can see you. Go!

You're back! Did you love it? Wasn't it the most psychedelic, fun and sometimes frightening film you have ever seen?

As a child, I had not read the book, so my first experience of Willy Wonka was on screen – and I'm not sure I took a breath or blinked during the whole film; I was just so immersed. It was like being in a trance. My dream for many years was for it all to be real, so I too could eat a daffodil, like Mr Wonka himself did, or drink chocolate from a river (but unlike Augustus Gloop, I would not fall in). I also remember having nightmares as a young boy, and I do think they were fuelled by the terrifying 'Tunnel of Terror' scene, when all the Golden Ticket winners are sailing along on the river of chocolate, only to find themselves speeding through a terrifying tunnel with scorpions and centipedes fighting it out in the background. I hid behind a cushion for that bit – and I still do. That scene does suggest a bit of a darker side to Mr Wonka, however, and I can relate to this, as many of us creatives have a darker side, which for me tends to manifest as a creative block when ideas are few and far between. Of course, this is temporary, and I soon get back to creating again, hopefully with more ideas and new trends to share.

Scary tunnels aside, the magic of the film has stayed with me ever since, and once I became a chocolatier, I was often called a real-life Willy Wonka.

We cannot ignore the amazing sweets and chocolates created by Willy Wonka: some did actually make their way to becoming real-life chocolate bars when Nestlé recreated a few, including the Scrumdiddlyumptious Chocolate Bar, with toffee, cookie and peanuts, and the Wonka Bar, with graham cracker pieces in milk chocolate. Nestlé Japan launched Wonka bars in two new flavours, the Whipple Scrumptious Caramel Delight and the Mysterious Spit-Spat Bar. Sadly, I missed all of these and hope one day they will be re-released so we can all try them.

Mr Wonka's fantastical inventions included Everlasting Gobstoppers, Three-Course Dinner Gum (which famously turned Violet Beauregard into a blueberry), Fizzy Lifting Drink (which brought drama when Charlie Bucket and Grandpa Joe drank some and floated towards the extractor fan, but managed to burp their way back to earth) and, my favourite, Lickable Wallpaper. Totally unhygienic, of course, but as a child, I just wanted my bedroom walls to be lickable and to taste of oranges.

Once I knew I wanted to become a chocolatier, my dreams of having a space like Willy Wonka's factory could not be recreated, as central London just didn't have a huge vacant factory space, nor I the budget. But I did live and work in my chocolaterie, with my own production kitchen, inventing new products every day, and making lots of people really happy, just like Willy Wonka. And although I didn't have any Oompa-Loompas, I did start to build a great team to help.

Charlie and the Chocolate Factory **(2005)** We cannot forget about Tim Burton's 2005 version, complete with Johnny Depp and CGI. This version, for me, is like a totally different experience, and I love it, but in a completely different way to the original.

It's surreal and funny, with the familiar super-vibrant saturation of colour wherever you look. It also has a lot of emotion, as Willy Wonka reveals a more vulnerable side and shares with us some of his childhood memories of not being allowed chocolate or sweets. It's fantastical and fast-paced, and of course, it's full of chocolate. It's a brillian updated version, but my heart is still with the original and always will be.

Chocolat **(2000)** Based on the novel by Joanne Harris, which we'll talk about in more detail on page 122, this film was a huge inspiration to me, as I saw it not long before I realised that I wanted to become a chocolatier. Being a chef, I have and had very little free time to read books apart from on holiday, so again, with *Chocolat*, I saw the film before reading the book. I watched it at the cinema with close friends, with no real idea of what to expect. From the moment it started, I didn't look away from the screen, not even to glance at or whisper to my friends. With muscle memory, I was able to eat a full sharing bag of chocolate without looking down or offering them to my companions. I felt an immediate connection to Vianne Rocher, the quiet village of Lansquenet-sous-Tannes and the travels Vianne and her daughter Anouk took, spreading her mother's secret cacao recipes. I could relate to the idea of moving house, going from town to town, village to village, as I was a restless soul in my twenties, having some inbuilt desire to see and experience as many places as I could. I counted that between the ages of 18 and 30, I had lived in 18 different houses and locations. I loved moving and travelling, but I was very focused on my goal of becoming a head pastry chef for Marco Pierre White. I achieved this in my late twenties, and it put a stop to all the moving around. My desire to travel did not disappear, however, and my love of fine chocolate had grown, so when the film was released, I felt a strong connection. From the moment the opening credits began, with swirling, winding music and the image of the small village, with Vianne and Anouk fighting against the winter wind, I knew I was in love and that it would be a film I would watch regularly for the rest of my life. The way I feel about *Chocolat* is so hard to express to you in writing, as it's a feeling that's very intense and unusual; a feeling I think we all get about something we feel fully part of, something bigger than you that that comes into your life at the right time. I will try, as I really want to express to you just how much it moulded the next twenty years of my life.

The film and book show a journey, not just of cacao, but of how cacao and chocolate bring people together, even when they don't initially accept one another. It's an intoxicating promise, something we eat and enjoy and give to others that always brings a smile, friendship and love. The process of Vianne building her new chocolaterie in the small, beautiful village was so motivating – and it's just what I did when I first started out. I even found a building with accommodation above, just like Vianne. Being a chocolatier means long hours making and creating. It's an intense commitment, and one I dove into so deeply that it really was my everything, even at the expense of seeing friends and family. That's where I do see a dramatic difference: Vianne made a connection with everyone in the village through her chocolate. I managed to do something similar in my first year of opening, but we had to expand and, in hindsight, that's where I lost my direct connection with people.

The film expresses indulgence, creativity, and the desire to create chocolates that will enhance people's lives and build connection. I could feel Vianne's obsession with cacao and how she embraced the supernatural as well as everyday human connection. Her kitchen could not have been more inspiring, although it would not be possible to achieve with today's strict food hygiene rules to follow! I do crave those rustic, earthy tones rather than the stark white and stainless-steel environment of commercial kitchens. I honestly believed I could smell the heavy, heady chocolate aromas coming from the cinema screen as the cacao beans were being broken and ground up to a liquid. I know it's a film, I know it was made to entertain, but I am a dreamer – one who tries really hard to make his dreams a reality – and this film planted a seed in my head, the dream that I would one day be doing the very same thing. And a few years later, I opened the doors of my very first chocolaterie.

I'm very much a visual person, so the film being my first experience of *Chocolat* was perfect: it deeply moves me and makes me feel inspired when I need a creative boost. Its colour palette, enchanting music and characters that are inspired by real people just bring me joy whenever I need it. Every time I watch the film, I get a little more from it, and I'm really glad that Joanne feels it is a sympathetic screenplay of her book. The book does have a darker side to it, so reading it after having seen the film was like embellishing on the story I already knew so well.

I'm 48 at the time of writing this book. The film is now 18 years old, so *Chocolat* now feels like my adopted child. I've watched it over 30 times in those 18 years, and it's never any less mesmerising to me.

Literature

***Chocolat* by Joanne Harris (1999)** The film and the book are two different entities for me, but they do connect, of course, and I feel they represent each other well. When any book is adapted into a film, there have to be changes and adjustments to make it visually striking and memorable. Because I watched the film before reading the book, I already had visuals from the film in my mind's eye when I was reading the book, which at times I needed to get out of my head to make it work. I have a very strong and clear way of thinking, and it's all visual; in fact, it's like watching a movie or another dimension of life playing alongside my reality. It can transport me to some pretty wonderful places, and if the writing is really descriptive, then my head builds up a moving picture so clear and crystalline that it's like I'm there while I'm reading. For me, this has to happen within the first paragraph of any book I read. If I'm there in that first paragraph, then I'm all in for the journey. Joanne Harris didn't just achieve this with her opening paragraph – she did it with her opening *sentence*: 'We came on the wind of the carnival.' The whole book is so descriptive and immersive, exactly what I expected and more. Joanne has kindly allowed me to use some of her own words, which perfectly sum up her astonishing book.

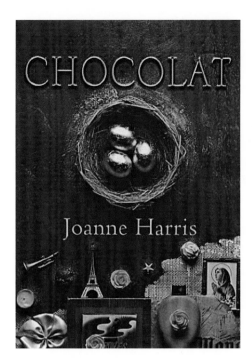

The original UK jacket of Joanne Harris's *Chocolat*, featuring three enticingly wrapped chocolate eggs.

Chocolat begins with the arrival in a tiny French village of Vianne Rocher, a single mother with a young daughter, on Shrove Tuesday. As the inhabitants of Lansquenet-sous-Tannes clear away the remains of the carnival that heralds the beginning of Lent, Vianne moves with her daughter into a disused bakery facing the church, where Francis Reynaud, the young and opinionated curé *of the parish, watches her arrival with disapproval and suspicion.*

When he realises that Vianne intends to open a chocolate shop in place of the old bakery, thereby tempting the churchgoers to over-indulgence, Reynaud's disapproval increases.

As it becomes clear that the villagers of Lansquenet are falling under the spell of Vianne's easy ways and unorthodox opinions, to the detriment of his own authority, he is quick to see her as a danger. Under Vianne's influence, an old woman embraces a new life, a battered wife finds the courage to leave her husband, children rebel against authority, outcasts and strays are welcomed … and Reynaud's tight and carefully ordered community is in danger of breaking apart. As Easter approaches, both parties throw themselves whole-heartedly into the preparations; Vianne for the chocolate festival she plans to hold on Easter Sunday, Reynaud into a desperate attempt to win back his straying flock. Both factions have a great deal at stake; the village is bitterly divided; and as the big day looms closer, their struggle becomes much more than a conflict between church and chocolate – it becomes an exorcism of the past, a declaration of independence, a showdown between dogma and understanding, pleasure and self-denial.

There are no real heroes or villains in Chocolat. *Even Reynaud, with his intransigence and his dark past, is more of a victim than an oppressor. His deep insecurity and his desire for order reflect Vianne's own need to belong, and her fear of being rejected. Nor is the Catholic Church the villain of the piece; Reynaud uses his own interpretation of Catholicism to enforce his own agenda of control and self-denial. Vianne does the same in a gentler way, but she too has preconceptions and prejudices, and like Reynaud, she is a victim of her past. I see Vianne and Reynaud as two sides of a single coin; closer in terms of their background, their fears and their struggle for dominance than anyone else in the story. To me, the real difference between them is that Vianne is a mother, whereas Reynaud, ironically, is a Father only in name.*

It's very hard to add any more to Joanne's wonderful words, other than to say that her book goes so much deeper than the film does, and in the novel, Vianne's belief in herself and her spirituality really draw me in. It's a dark, seductive chocolate rather than a sweet love story – and it's just wonderfully immersive and captivating.

Grendel: A Cautionary Tale About Chocolate by David Lucas (2013)

I love a good children's story book: the colourful illustrations and simplicity of the words always make me smile. We tend to stop reading children's books as we age, but I'm thinking we should pick one up every now and again and be transported back to the dream worlds they contain. It can remind us of being very young and the things we used to wish for, like *I wish fizzy pop came out of the tap instead of water, I wish it would rain chocolate, I wish EVERYTHING was made of chocolate*. I remember wishing for all of these things as a child. Imagine my excitement when I realised that fizzy pop *did* come out of a tap in pubs and restaurants – and that you *can* (sort of) have everything made of chocolate, but only in a controlled exhibition-style setting: fun, but not quite my wish come true.

Grendel tells the story of young monster (called Grendel). He lives with his mum and pet dog in their cave. Grendel loves chocolate, and would eat it all day if he could. His mum buys Grendel a chocolate egg and, without a second thought, he rushes off to his hiding place to scoff the lot. Inside the egg he finds a note granting Grendel three wishes. Of course, he wishes for more chocolate, and from the sky falls lots of chocolate. His second wish is for everything he touches to turn to chocolate – a little bit like King Midas turning everything into gold. The log he is sitting on, the leaves he touches, the ground he walks on, all became chocolate. And – brace yourselves – Grendel gives his dog a hug, turning him into chocolate too. When his mum approaches, she suffers the same fate. With the sun shining brightly and his mum beginning to melt, Grendel remembers he has one more wish. After a lot of thought, he wishes himself back to yesterday. *Very clever, Grendel*. He wakes up to find everything back to normal, and his mum gives him the chocolate egg once again. This time, he gives it to her, telling her to think very carefully about the wishes. I laughed hard at the final page, as she wishes for a huge pet dragon. Very cool indeed. The moral of the story is great, and the illustrations really take me back to my early childhood. So, enjoy your chocolate, but in moderation – and always share. Well, nearly always.

Chocolate: The Definitive Guide by Sara Jayne-Stanes (1999)

I had to include this book as it's so thoroughly researched, and was written by someone so passionate about chocolate that it became part of her life's work. Sara became a good friend and supporter of my work from the very beginning, and we shared many fantastic moments of chocolate tasting together as part of the Academy of Chocolate, of which she was one of the founders and chairwoman. We also had some disagreements too, about which chocolate was better than the other, or which truffle had the right texture or flavour, yet we never allowed this to taint our friendship. In fact, being able to debate so openly was quite refreshing. As I was writing this book, I received the very sad news that Sara had passed away after a period of illness. She leaves a huge hole in the culinary and chocolate industry. However, she also leaves us with her acclaimed book, *Chocolate: The Definitive Guide*. If you want to read in depth about the history and timeline of cacao, then hunt a copy down. This was my bible in my early days of discovering the story behind cacao and chocolate.

Reading Sara's book, you immediately understand her passion for fine chocolate: it's clear from the way she writes. For example: 'Chocolate is unique. The main secret of its exquisite pleasure is that it is the only substance to melt at blood temperature, gently exploding into a warm, sensual liquid, filling your mouth with an incomparable hedonistic feeling that is so delicious you just want to go on savouring it.' Is this the most wonderful description of how we all experience all chocolate? Yes, I think it is – and so perfectly written that I'm not going to try to rewrite it. Her book is a journey from pod to palate, with a detailed timeline of cacao from 5000 BCE to 2000 CE, as well as covering how chocolate is made. Then there's a wonderful collection of chocolate recipes, including one of my all-time favourite recipes of Sara's: her version of Death by Chocolate. It's wildly decadent and totally unapologetic, as Sara did not suffer nor tolerate food guilt. She just believed in eating great-quality chocolate, and making all your recipes with great ingredients.

Her signature chocolates were Nipples of Venus, for which she had a secret recipe. I've made my own version on page 132, with the aim of celebrating the life of Sara and her intoxicating drive and passion for cacao.

Music

'Chocolate' – Kylie Minogue (2004) In 2004, I knew I wanted to change my career and go from being a pastry chef to dipping myself in the world of fine chocolate. With *Chocolat* (the film and book) still fresh in my mind, Kylie's top-ten hit 'Chocolate' came at the perfect time. The stars were clearly aligned and coming together for me. I believe everything we are meant to do is built up by different ingredients that show us the way to what we really want, so you could say I felt this was another sign for me to change my direction. The song was part of her 2003 album *Body Language*, an awesome album (and yes, I say that about all of Kylie's albums, as I'm a massive fan. Squeal!) If you have not watched the video or heard the song, then this is your cue. Absorb, immerse and disappear for 4 minutes, as it's wonderfully rich. Don't forget to have a piece of chocolate to melt in your mouth as you listen; it's an experiential moment. See you in 4.

How was it? Wonderful, right? And the song is all about love, our addiction to love and the absolutely uncontrollable way chocolate and love consume us, distract us, entice us and seduce us. We love chocolate, we have a relationship with chocolate, and the song says it all. For me, this song is like allowing a dark chocolate cream truffle to melt on my tongue: slowly, carefully, and with absolute surrender to its rich, silky seductiveness. The song *is* melted chocolate; it has sounds of deep soul, electronic high notes and orchestral waves. That's what I think chocolate sounds like when it's being melted, mixed and swirled around. In the video, the dancers are like elegant ballerinas, but I always think of them as the chocolates in a luxurious satin-lined box, all the same flavour, and in the centre of the box is one chocolate wrapped in burgundy satin (or maybe foil) and everyone wants it. It's not for sharing; it's the rare and wonderful chocolate that will make you fall in love. It will seduce you, melt you and take you on a journey – and this chocolate is Kylie herself.

As I've said, I am a dreamer, and I spent months visualising my new chocolate shop – and, more importantly, its grand opening – and yes, I did visualise Kylie singing at the opening with her dancers mesmerising all the guests. I still do, and one day I will have a space that is grand, huge, a walk-in chocolate box, and Kylie will be there, singing the song that I played and replayed in my head over and over. I might not have had Kylie at the launch of my first shop, or the second, third or fourth, but I did have my business partner, family and friends, and Kylie was playing in my head all evening, with those luxurious sounds and dance moves helping as I set out on the vibrant and consuming journey ahead of me.

'Sweet Like Chocolate' – Shanks and Bigfoot (1999) I love music and always have. I play brass, learned to read music at a very early age and, with help from my mum, who is a pianist and violinist, I was able to appreciate so many genres of music and loved to play them. There are some sounds I don't gravitate towards, though, and when this song was released, it was one of them. It came out in 1999 and topped the UK chart for two weeks, before going on to be a huge hit in Australia, New Zealand, Ireland and across Europe. At the time, I definitely did not know I would one day become a chocolatier, but I was a head pastry chef and anything sweet in popular culture was on my radar. I remember this song playing so much every day in my pastry kitchen in the heart of Soho, London. The one thing that helped us get through the workload was music, and we knew every song in the charts.

Even though I didn't really like it, this song has stuck in my head, mainly because of the music video. The whole thing is an animation of a girl with pigtails on an open-topped double-decker bus. All the other passengers are chocolate biscuits, and everything around her is made of chocolate. She visits a chocolate factory, then ventures into the countryside with dancing insects. It's a song of love and how sweet falling in love

Did you know?
The blood in the shower scene of Alfred Hitchcock's *Psycho* was actually chocolate syrup.

THE JOY OF CHOCOLATE

with someone is, addictive and full of joy. The perfect theme for a song, and using something we all fall in love with as the metaphor is genius. To say that someone is as sweet as chocolate is the best way to say 'I love you'. Right?

'Chocolate' – The 1975 (2013) Try not to dance when you listen to 'Chocolate' by The 1975: it's impossible, I promise you. It makes you smile so much, so if you are having a bit of a down day, then listen to this.

The song was released in March 2013 as part of their *Music for Cars* EP, and also appeared on their self-titled debut album. So, is the song about chocolate? Well, I did think it was, until I did a bit of digging after it had been around for a few months and realised that 'chocolate' is being used as a code word for 'cannabis', which then makes total sense when you listen to the lyrics. I'm sure the police would not be worried if you were eating a Twix, or if your car smelled of chocolates. When you think about it, though, they are both addictive and can be really hard to give up, so using chocolate as an alternative word is pretty clever, really – plus it makes the song more approachable and safer for young listeners.

Art

Amaury Guichon It's very difficult to find the words to explain how skilled Amaury is with chocolate and pastry: the incredible chocolate sculptures he creates are off-the-scale, mind-blowing stuff. You can see his stunning work on social media, or even sign up to take a course with him in Los Angeles, USA, where he is based. Chocolate can be challenging to work with, so when someone makes it look like anything is possible, you sit up and take notice, and lose hours and hours watching their videos. At least, that's what I did when I found Amaury and his work on Instagram. Usually, I like chocolate to still look like chocolate, even when it's sculpted and constructed into lifelike things, but I will set that opinion aside for the moment. Amaury's work comes to life with skilful airbrushing and cocoa-butter spraying. It's clear to see the dedication he puts in to delivering some of the finest and cleverest chocolate sculptures on the planet. You don't have to be a chocolatier or pastry chef to be wowed and mesmerised by the techniques and finishes he uses; it's simply joyous to watch.

I will focus on one particular piece of work I love by Amaury, as the subject is already interesting to me, so the idea of creating it with chocolate just elevates my interest even more. I love funfairs of all kinds, and I love all the rides. Amaury has created a working Ferris wheel, of which every component part is chocolate. It's so skilfully crafted, and I'm blown away by how the delicate rods and wires of chocolate do not break. It's the precision of his measuring and his astonishing attention to detail that allows this to work. It looks like a scale model from a vintage fairground, a real Ferris wheel you want to jump on and ride. The colour palette is red, gold and white, with small details that make it authentic and so realistic. Amaury's videos are full of smiles, and his final masterpieces always make me smile too; I'm there with him in spirit, full of joy for what he can create with his hands and some very clever problem-solving.

Prudence Emma Staite A chocolate motorbike, chocolate celebrity portraits and a working chocolate pub bar are just some of the hundreds of things Prudence has created out of chocolate. Her company, Food is Art, isn't just about chocolate, though. Prudence can use food to create pretty much anything, including a life-sized replica of the Greek statue *Discobolus* out of cheese. I first met Prudence when helping organise the Chocolate Ball charity event for CLIC Sargent (now called Young Lives vs Cancer). She really pulled out the stops with an entire sitting room made from chocolate, including edible skirting boards, all made by hand. With commissions from world-famous chocolate brands you may have seen Prudence's work in adverts, on TV and in magazines, so I asked her where she gets her inspiration and ideas. Here's what she had to say.

I have been creating all types of artworks with different foods for nearly 20 years, but my first passion was working with chocolate to make interactive and edible art. I love working with chocolate – there are so many ways you can work with it, from painting with it to sculpting it like clay. I am always looking at different ways to explore chocolate and, over the years, I have built some really large installations with chocolate, including an entire pop-up bar dispensing beer in chocolate glasses.

One of my favourite projects was creating a life-sized replica of a vintage AJS motorcycle. Having no real knowledge of motorcycles, I had to study and learn all about them to ensure that the chocolate version was correct, even down to the correct dimensions of the nuts and bolts. The sculpture used 120kg (265 lb) of chocolate and took 2 months to hand-sculpt. It featured a solid chocolate engine; chocolate nuts, bolts and springs all sprayed with edible silver to give a realistic finish; a seat made from chocolate that was textured to look like real leather; and a chocolate oil can, filled with liquid chocolate and with its own oil spill made by refracting light in chocolate.

A lot of my works are multi-sensory, but don't include sound, so I wanted to explore the idea of making something in chocolate that you could hear as well as see, touch, smell and taste. After a lot of experimenting, I was able to make a chocolate record that could be played on a turntable: it's chocolate that engages all the above-mentioned senses, and also includes movement – you can dance to it and then eat it!

The first artwork I created was a chocolate portrait with a solid chocolate canvas, chocolate paint and a chocolate frame painted with an edible gold colour – so it was an entirely edible creation. Over the years, I have created many of these portraits. I also use chocolate shapes and buttons to make edible mosaics of all sizes, and create solid chocolate life-sized sculptures of people.

I relish the thrill of a challenge, and can't wait to find out what other exciting projects will come up in the future.

Myself for Jo Malone London (2021) I had not originally planned to include myself in this chapter, but I was asked to create piece of chocolate art with the brief of 'My Spring' by world-famous perfume brand Jo Malone London, and I'm so proud of what I eventually created that I had to share it with you all. My work was featured alongside that of a wonderful group of artists in what would have been a public exhibition, but due to the COVID-19 lockdown, it became an online exhibition. I wanted to make my work sensory, and my first seed of an idea was smell. I identified some key elements of spring I love: a cherry blossom tree in our garden at home; new buds and soft green leaves on trees; the first smell and feeling of the sun's warmth after the winter's biting grip. The result was four spheres made from chocolate, each smelling of a different element of spring. One was a sphere of cherry blossom, fragrant with a sweet perfume; next a sphere of fresh green leaves, verdant and newborn; then a warm sphere of the sun's rays, smelling of warm earth and pavement; and finally, all three muddled together in a chocolate terrazzo sphere: spring in its entirety.

The first attempt was a disaster. It was twisted, gnarled and knobbly, like a Halloween tree with green buds, so into the bin it went – it did not spark joy. Cherry blossom took centre stage after the first

My four chocolate sculptures of 'My Spring' for Jo Malone London, Spring Artist Series 2021. From left to right, Cherry Blossom, The Sun's Warmth, Total Spring and New Shoots and Leaves.

CHOCOLATE IN POPULAR CULTURE

disaster of green leaves, and this style set the tone for the rest of the spheres: clean lines and slightly cartoon-like, 1960s-style prints. Next I made the green leaves sphere and the sun sphere, both with a similar style and character, but all smelling so different, as I used essential oils to bring them to life with fragrance. My idea was to have all four spheres displayed under large glass domes with a smelling hole in the top so guests could breathe in my spring and visualise those lovely warming and lively days of growth before summer. This project was a joy to work on and I'm really excited to be able to share it with you. The picture was taken by my photographer partner, Luke, and I'm thrilled with the result. I hope you enjoy them as much as I did making them.

Patrick Roger Patrick is a world-famous French chocolatier and chocolate sculptor. I love his work, and when my first book, *Adventures with Chocolate*, was being published in French, Patrick agreed to write the preface. These were my early days in the chocolate industry, so this was a huge deal for me and still is. Patrick makes wonderful chocolates, but it's his unique style of sculpting that really captured my fascination. The first sculpture I saw in his Paris boutique was of an orangutan crouching over. It was pretty arresting and caught everyone's attention. To explain why this is such an important piece of work is hard: it's not just a chocolate orangutan. I will start with the finish Patrick achieves on the surface, which is deeply textural and tonal. No colours are sprayed on, which I love, as the chocolate in all its wonderful tones of brown tells the story of this piece. You can see Patrick's hands in his work: he uses his fingernails to create texture, his strength to push and carve the chocolate as he creates such lifelike features. The orangutan has such an interesting face, a face that has lived and has stories to tell. It's a still piece, but with so much vigour and life that it's hard not to feel as though it will move and breathe at any moment. The way Patrick can manipulate chocolate to fall, suspend and be still, yet with so much movement, is remarkable.

Recipes inspired by popular culture

It's a joy to be able to share with you five recipes inspired by these fantastic chocolate moments in popular culture. They are my expression of what I feel those moments should be like, and I wanted to make them achievable for you at home: so have fun making them, and just enjoy how much chocolate is part of our everyday lives.

Kylie's chocolate

This is such a sexy love song: it sounds as smooth as caramel, as creamy as milk chocolate and as intoxicating as a fine dessert wine, syrupy and viscous with a long, satisfying finish. I want to capture this in a truffle that makes you feel swept up with a silky-smooth decadence, loved, seduced and thoroughly spoiled by the texture, taste and aromas. It's a love affair: a secret one you may wish to keep for yourself, for those days, moments and times when it's just you making time stand still for a few moments. You will be very surprised at how easy these are to make: nothing complicated or fussy, just buy fantastic-quality chocolate that you love enough not to share, as this is your chocolate and yours only. This recipe is about time taken for you when you need to stop, breathe and love yourself, totally and fully. Kylie, thank you for the wonderful song. I hope you think of it when you sit down and enjoy these entirely provocative and sexy truffles.

Mix the cream, sugar and sea salt together in a small saucepan over a medium heat and warm, stirring, until the cream simmers and all the sugar and salt have dissolved.

Place the chopped chocolate in a mixing bowl. Pour half of the warm cream mixture over it and mix well. Once combined, add the remaining cream and mix with a whisk to emulsify. Take care not to beat it with the whisk, as we do not want any air incorporated into the ganache.

Once it's wonderfully glossy, mix in the butter cubes, stirring until they are fully incorporated.

Refrigerate for 2 hours.

When you're ready to continue, scoop out nuggets of ganache at your desired size and leave them rough and uneven: perfect imperfection.

Scatter the cocoa powder in a shallow dish and roll the truffles in the powder to coat, then place on a serving plate or dish and enjoy at room temperature.

They can be stored in the fridge in an airtight container for up to 2 weeks.

Makes 50 small truffles or 25 indulgent–sized truffles

For the ganache
350ml (12fl oz) double cream
150g (5oz) unrefined light muscovado sugar
¼ teaspoon sea salt flakes
300g (10½oz) dark chocolate (at least 75 per cent cocoa solids), chopped into small pieces
50g (1¾oz) unsalted butter, cut into cubes

For rolling the ganache
100g (3½oz) cocoa powder

Nipples of Venus

Not a chocolate you will find easily in chocolate shops, nor in your mainstream chocolate box, which is so sad, as this is a stunning chocolate and always comes with a cheeky smile. I've always known and loved this seductive chocolate, and when I saw it featured in *Chocolat*, with Juliette Binoche as Vianne offering one to the steely Comte de Reynaud, I screamed out with joy.

A stunning blend of sweet chestnut and brandy with a buttery finish, enrobed in white chocolate with dark chocolate decoration: you will fall in love with this recipe. If you want another film reference, these chocolates also make a seductive appearance in the wild and lavish 1984 film *Amadeus*. It's a wonderfully creative and immersive movie to watch while eating your homemade nipples.

To make the filling

Line a baking tray with baking paper.

Place the dark chocolate in a heatproof bowl set over a pan of hot water and melt until heated to 50°C (122°F). Take it off the heat and allow to cool for 5 minutes.

In a stand mixer with a paddle attachment, cream together the butter and sugar until light in colour.

In a food processor, purée the chestnuts until they are as fine as possible, then mix them into the creamed butter and sugar. Add the brandy and mix well, and finally add the melted chocolate, mixing well once again.

If the mix seems a little too soft, allow it to stand until it's a good piping consistency. Fill a piping bag with the mixture and cut a 2cm (¾in) hole at the tip.

Pipe peaked kisses of the mixture on to the prepared baking tray and refrigerate for 30 minutes.

To enrobe and decorate

Using a chocolate dipping fork or kitchen fork, dip the kisses into the tempered white chocolate, tapping off any excess. Return the coated kisses to the lined tray and allow them to set fully.

Recipe continues overleaf

Makes 30 nipples

For the filling

220g (7¾oz) dark chocolate (65–70 per cent cocoa solids)

5 tablespoons unsalted butter

40g (1½oz) unrefined golden caster sugar

450g (1lb) vacuum-packed chestnuts

100ml (3½fl oz) brandy

1 teaspoon vanilla extract

For enrobing and decoration

400g (14oz) white chocolate, tempered according to the instructions on pages 63 or 84

50g (1¾oz) dark or ruby chocolate (at least 70 per cent cocoa solids)

To decorate, melt the dark or ruby chocolate in a heatproof bowl set over a pan of hot water. Once it is cool but still liquid, dip the very tips of the nipples into the chocolate and shake off any excess. Return to the tray once and allow to set.

Enjoy your nipples of Venus at room temperature — and never refrigerate, as there isn't a nipple anywhere that loves cold temperatures.

෨ **To add more joy** An easy and beautiful way to present the nipples is to cut squares of tissue paper or baking paper and crumple them around the nipples, then place them in a vintage box or tin.

Did you know?
'Military chocolate' has been included in the ration packs of US soldiers since 1937, as it provides both morale and an energy boost.

Botanical bonbons

My creative work for Jo Malone London cemented my love of using botanicals in chocolate and showed how nature can be transposed so well into flavour and texture. Take some time to explore the nature around you, wherever you are in the world. Seek out the wild-growing edibles on offer, such as herbs, florals, leaves, berries and grasses such as hay. Please take advice if you are not sure what is edible and safe, or, like I do, use pure distilled essential oils that are safe to ingest alongside the things I'm confident in using. These include lavender, kitchen herbs, geranium, lemon balm, ylang-ylang, jasmine and lemongrass. You can blend so many florals and herbs together and easily build a wonderfully colourful and fragrant combination. Bonbons are really just truffles; however, I've made these smaller and rolled them in fragrant sugar to give them a crunchy, crystallised coating, making them sweeter and more intense in flavour.

To make the decoration sugar

Begin by making the decoration sugar so it has time to infuse. Simply mix the sugar and lemongrass together and leave to infuse in a sealed jar or a bowl covered with clingfilm. This will create a beautiful lemongrass–flavoured sugar for the decoration.

To make the ganache

Place the water, mint, lemon thyme, lavender and sugar in a small saucepan over a medium heat. Bring to a simmer until the sugar dissolves completely, then strain half of the sugar syrup into a bowl containing the chopped chocolate. Whisk until glossy, then strain in the remaining syrup and mix well to create your ganache.

Allow to cool, then refrigerate for 2 hours.

To enrobe and finish

When you're ready to continue, line a baking tray with baking paper.

Take your chilled ganache and divide it into 50 pieces. Roll them all into balls using your hands, dusting a little cocoa powder on your fingers if the ganache starts to melt.

Recipe continues overleaf

Makes approximately 50 bonbons

For the ganache

175ml (6fl oz) water
15g (½oz) mint leaves and stems
15g (½oz) lemon thyme leaves
10g (¼oz) edible dried lavender flowers
100g (3½oz) unrefined golden caster sugar
400g (14oz) dark chocolate (60 per cent cocoa solids)
5 drops of jasmine essential oil
20g (¾oz) cocoa powder

For enrobing the bonbons

250g (9oz) dark chocolate (60 per cent cocoa solids), tempered according to the instructions on pages 63 or 84

For the decoration sugar

unrefined golden caster sugar
1 lemongrass stalk, chopped

CHOCOLATE IN POPULAR CULTURE

Sift the lemongrass sugar into a shallow bowl. The sugar will be perfectly infused, and the lemongrass can be used in to infuse more sugar, or added to your next Thai green curry.

Roll the bonbons in the tempered chocolate. Start with a thin layer, placing them on the lined tray to set.

Once set, repeat for a second layer of chocolate coating, then roll through the lemongrass sugar until the balls are fully coated. This is easier if you have a friend to help you.

Once coated in sugar, leave them to set fully for 10 minutes before transferring to their presentation box or bowl, where you will need to leave them to rest for an hour so they come to room temperature. Finally, taste and enjoy a very botanical, floral and fragrant chocolate.

Chocolate-orange death by chocolate

My version of Sara's death by chocolate

When you read this recipe and make the cake, you may think it's just another chocolate cake, but you are mistaken. It's not *just* a chocolate cake. It's the most chocolatey chocolate cake there is, with more filling than you feel there should be, but that's what gives it its name. Will it actually kill you? Is it too much to enjoy? No, of course not. It's a classic, and now it's your classic. It's everything you could want when you need indulgence, when you have friends visiting, or just when life feels too much, and a spot of baking and chocolate making is all the therapy you need.

To make the cake

Preheat the oven to 175°C/155°C fan/345°F/gas 3½ and line the base and sides of a loose-bottomed 25cm(10in) round cake tin with silicone baking paper.

In a heatproof bowl set over a pan of hot water, melt together the chocolate, sugars, butter and orange juice. Once combined, take off the heat and mix in the orange zest, egg yolks, vanilla extract and creme fraiche until smooth.

Add the flour, bicarbonate of soda, salt and cream of tartar, and whisk to combine.

In a separate bowl, whisk the egg whites until they reach soft peak stage, then fold them in to the chocolate mixture to create a light, fluffy batter.

Spoon the batter into your lined cake tin and bake in the middle of the oven for 45 minutes. If the cake is done a skewer should come out clean.If not, bake for a further few minutes. Remove from the oven and allow the cake to rest in the tin for 10 minutes before carefully lifting it out on to a wire rack to cool completely.

To make the the chocolate-orange filling

Melt together the chocolates and butter in a saucepan over a low heat. Add the sea salt and orange oil and mix well until smooth and glossy. Set aside to cool.

For the cake

225g (8oz) dark chocolate (70 per cent cocoa solids)

125g (4½oz) unrefined light muscovado sugar

100g (3½oz) unrefined golden caster sugar

115g (4oz) unsalted butter

150ml (5fl oz) freshly squeezed orange juice

zest of 2 oranges

2 medium free-range eggs, separated

1 teaspoon vanilla extract

150ml (5fl oz) full-fat creme fraiche

225g (8oz) plain flour

½ teaspoon bicarbonate of soda

½ teaspoons crushed sea salt flakes

1 teaspoon cream of tartar

To make the syrup

Combine the sugar and water in a small saucepan over a high heat. Bring to a simmer, stirring well so all the sugar dissolves. Allow to cool completely, then add the orange liqueur.

To assemble

Once your cake is completely cool, slice through it to create three even layers. Carefully separate them out.

Now brush each cake layer with a generous amount of the syrup, using it all up.

Re-line the bottom and sides of your cake tin with silicone baking paper and place the bottom layer of cake into the tin. Divide the filling into two halves and spread the first half over the cake layer in the tin. Place the next cake layer on top and press to level. Spoon over the remaining filling, then smooth it out and top with the final layer of chocolate cake, pressing it down firmly.

Refrigerate for 30 minutes.

To make the coating

Meanwhile, make the coating. Bring the cream to a simmer in a saucepan over a medium heat. Place the chopped chocolate in a heatproof bowl and pour the cream over the top. Add the orange oil and mix well, then allow to cool to a thick, spreadable icing.

Remove the cake from the tin and mix the coating well before smothering it all over the cake – do not worry about being neat.

To decorate

Lay out a sheet of baking paper on the worktop. Spread the tempered chocolate over the top and, just before it sets fully, use a sharp knife to cut it into long thin strips of chocolate. Leave to set fully, then remove the paper and attach the strips of chocolate around the top edge of the cake. Dust with cocoa powder and serve at room temperature, with pouring cream or creme fraiche.

For the chocolate–orange filling
375g (13oz) dark chocolate
    (70 per cent cocoa solids)
150g (5oz) milk chocolate
    (40 per cent cocoa solids)
425g (15oz) unsalted butter
½ teaspoon crushed sea salt
    flakes
1 teaspoon orange oil (pure oil
    of orange, not orange essence
    or flavouring)

For the syrup
100g (3½oz) unrefined golden
    caster sugar
100ml (3½fl oz) water
50ml (2fl oz) orange liqueur

For the coating
250ml (9fl oz) whipping cream
250g (9oz) dark chocolate
    (70 per cent cocoa solids),
    chopped
½ teaspoon orange oil
    (see above)

For the decoration
250g (9oz) dark chocolate
    (70 per cent cocoa solids),
    tempered according to the
    instructions on pages 63 or 84
20g (¾oz) cocoa powder

Did you know?
Referring to chocolate, Spanish conquistador Hernán Cortés declared that 'A cup of this precious drink permits a man to walk for a whole day without food.'

CHOCOLATE IN POPULAR CULTURE

Charlie's chocolate bar

Willy Wonka created all the chocolates and sweets in both films, and I've always wondered what Charlie would make if he had the opportunity to create his own chocolate bar. So this is me having fun, and imagining that I'm Charlie, stepping back into the chocolate factory now that it's his. I think Charlie would go all out and create the most wonderfully over-the-top bar of chocolate ever. You will need a deep chocolate bar mould for this, or you can use a small, shallow rectangular plastic food container. The quantities of filling will depend on how big your bar moulds are and how many you make, so feel free to decide how much of each you want to include.

You will want to fill your bar or food container with quite a thick layer of chocolate so that you have a cavity to stuff with all the filling ingredients. To do this, fill the mould with chocolate and tap out the air bubbles. Let the mould sit for 2–3 minutes, then tip out any excess chocolate, leaving a thick shell of chocolate behind in the mould. Save any remaining chocolate and use your hairdryer to keep it fluid yet still tempered.

Place the mould in the fridge for 15 minutes, then remove the shell from the bar mould or food container and place on a wire rack.

For the first layer of filling, spoon peanut butter into the chocolate shell until it's about one third full, then sprinkle over some of the chocolate chip cookie chunks. Pipe or spoon on some caramel to fill by another third, then leave to set for an hour.

Now fill the rest of the bar with mini marshmallows, pretzels and brownie pieces, being generous and allowing the pieces stick up in a way that looks spiky and architectural.

Spoon over the remaining tempered milk chocolate to fully enrobe and cover the bar and its filling. Tap the wire rack to remove any excess chocolate.

Lift the bar off the rack and on to a tray lined with baking paper. Refrigerate for 10 minutes.

We eat with our eyes, so a little decorating is needed to make them really pop. Use the melted white chocolate to pipe a series of very fine lines across one end of the bar. Always eat at room temperature, and always share them with only the people you love or want to impress.

For the bar mould and coating
500g (1lb 2oz) milk chocolate, tempered according to the instructions on pages 63 or 84 melted

For the filling
peanut butter
chocolate chip cookies, broken into small chunks
caramel sauce (dulce de leche or caramelised condensed milk)
mini marshmallows
pretzels, broken into pieces
brownies, broken into small chunks

To decorate
white chocolate, melted

Festivals, rituals and celebrations

The human race's devotion to chocolate and the cacao bean means we have found many different ways to celebrate this wonderful gift across the world, from chocolate ceremonies to thank the gods to the (rather gruesome) past rituals of the Maya people, which are thankfully not practised today. Chocolate festivals are held all around the world, with hundreds of thousands of visitors wanting to taste the latest chocolatiers' creations and learn about new cacao bean varieties, plantations and secrets. And then there are all the personal and sometimes private rituals each of us has around chocolate, from a chocolate martini enjoyed in the bubble bath at the end of a long week, to carefully shaping the wrappers from a selection box into a miniature sculpture as we eat.

So, it's festival time, carnival time: time to celebrate and share our global love of cacao and chocolate and learn about the different ways in which people come together to taste, eat and enjoy all things chocolate.

Cacao ceremonies and rituals

We have been celebrating chocolate for thousands of years across the globe, with the same respect and joy for the beloved cacao bean demonstrated across the centuries.

Although discovered by the Olmecs in 1500 BC, it is the Maya and the Aztecs that have received the most spotlight when we look at how they celebrated and prized cacao. Both peoples believed that cacao was discovered by the gods on a mountain and then gifted to them. The Maya held a yearly festival to honour the cacao god Ek Chuah, which included several offerings and rituals to him. Both the Maya and the Aztecs prized cacao and held it in such high regard that their rituals became legendary, with human sacrifices playing a role in their thanks to the gods. In essence, Maya legends and mythology state that they believed they were partially created with cacao, and that cacao was in their blood.

The beans we now know and love were used as currency by the Aztecs and the Maya, with the colour of the beans in part determining their value: the lighter or ashy beans were more valuable than the darker, shrivelled beans, and it's now believed that there were four categories of bean beans used in bartering and buying. I love the thought of bartering with cacao: one chocolate bar for a box of eggs, or a box of handmade chocolates for a bottle of good wine. I wonder, could we make this work today?

Cacao ceremonies and rituals have been part of the cacao bean's history for thousands of years, and they are catching our attention once again, especially among those of us who find ourselves overworked, stressed and burned out. The cacao ceremonies of the ancient Mesoamerican cultures involved comforting and cheering those who were about to be sacrificed. Thankfully, today we do not partake in this practice, but you can still experience a cacao ceremony ritual for yourself. Cacao is classed as a medicinal ingredient for many healers around the world, but it has to be pure and of fine quality, not from a mass-market bar of dark chocolate.

So, what is a cacao ceremony? You may think this is too spiritual for you, but if you put this in the same context as a group of friends having a coffee or beer together, sharing thoughts and experiences and connecting, then you will get on just great with a cacao ceremony. Cacao in its purest form – as just the bean blended with water – is pretty powerful stuff. It can give you a sense of euphoria, making you feel lifted, happy and connected with those around you as your frequencies align. I'm going to let an expert explain in more detail: my healer, Tijen.

Tijen is a spiritual healer and owner of White Aura Holistic Healing in Potters Bar, just outside London, UK. She is a reiki master and a frequency and spiritual healer, and she uses the cacao ceremony as part of her group breathing work sessions. I've asked Tijen to explain her first cacao ceremony and the benefits of experiencing a ceremony of this type. Here's what she had to say:

My first experience of a cacao ceremony was during some dark times I had been experiencing. I was 'soul searching', looking for holistic ways to deal with my anxiety and depression. Cacao ceremonies weren't something I was familiar with; however, after having heard cacao was classed as a plant medicine and Amazonian superfood, I was up for trying! A group of around five of us came together during a full moon meditation circle. We shared what we were grateful for, we meditated, and we worked on letting go of past issues, fear and negative emotions. I was offered a cacao drink, which was blended with some fresh coconut milk, coconut sugar, and a few drops of essential oils. I fell in love, and soon started to research more to try and understand the many healing properties cacao holds for us on both a physical and spiritual level.

After studying its historical use during shamanic healing ceremonies, I learned that it was used as a medicinal plant, and it soon became a big part of my life, my diet and the work I do now. I often offer it in my healing and meditation circles to assist with rooting and rebalancing the energies within us, and to restore good health. These circles often involve opening up to complete strangers about our experiences, but the cacao helps creates a safe and intimate space where everyone's fears, hopes, suffering and dreams can be shared. We often find we all have similar problems and fears, as well as hopes for our lives. Drinking the cacao together helps us to open up. It enables us to hear our true selves and work through blockages and past traumas, as well as to dissolve any pent-up negative emotions and align us with who we truly are.

Cacao is packed with so many vitamins and minerals that are great for cardiovascular health and emotional wellbeing. It is renowned for releasing dopamine and endorphins, which soothe depression by boosting the mood. Cacao also contains anandamide, which is known as 'the bliss molecule'. This is the same thing produced in our bodies when we work out and feel a rush of good energy. It also balances blood sugar levels, and creates more blood flow to the brain, helping to strengthen awareness and focus.

Spiritually, cacao is renowned for opening the heart, and allowing us to connect with ourselves and others in a deeper way than before. Any fear that is currently taking hold of us will be replaced with love and joy. It helps strengthen our connection to our higher selves, which in turn connects us to our own inner power, strength and truth.

The cacao ceremony gives my clients the opportunity to connect to their inner spirits, which helps them to explore meditation on a much deeper and spiritual level, as well helping them to focus and be in the present with more ease. Cacao is also used to bring inspiration and creativity together, helping us move past those inner blocks that keep us disconnected from our creative life force. It's truly a life-changing experience to drink cacao with intention while appreciating the power it holds to heal us.

I am yet to experience a cacao ceremony for myself, but as a way to experience more joy in our lives, it sounds pretty fantastic – and it shows that cacao is still as important in rituals today as it was thousands of years ago.

Chocolate festivals

Another way in which we can all celebrate chocolate and the cacao bean is to visit a chocolate festival. These are usually consumer shows where cacao growers, chocolate producers and chocolatiers are able to come together in order to showcase the very best of all things chocolate. They are a safe place to geek out and explore,

ChocolART, Germany's biggest chocolate festival, takes place in Tübingen. The celebration of chocolate includes a market, cooking courses, lectures and more.

and the perfect way to learn everything there is to know about the industry, from growing cacao to selling chocolates. Plus, of course, you can purchase pretty much any type of chocolate and build your own library of chocolate bars. I have had the privilege of visiting and exhibiting at many different wonderful chocolate shows around the world.

Here's a travel tip for you: next time you plan a holiday, look at where cacao grows, or look at where chocolate is really popular, and you will find a chocolate festival taking place; you can go to Grenada, Perugia, Paris, Tokyo, London, Amsterdam or Seattle. These are a small slice of the chocolate festivals you should put on your travel app. They all share one aim: to introduce as many people as possible to fine cacao and chocolate.

I absolutely love a chocolate festival. There will always be something wonderful to discover: a new chocolate maker, a new chocolate bar, a chocolatier with a new collection of divine truffles to taste ... wherever you look, you will see hundreds or thousands of visitors with very smiley faces. You will not find this an unhappy or stressful place. The visitors are there to taste and forage their way through all the exhibitors, all led by the same intoxicating desire to discover their new favourite piece of chocolate. These festivals really are places of joy and happiness.

Did you know?
The world's most visited chocolate festival is Salon du Chocolat, with shows around the globe, including a fashion show where the world's top chocolatiers and pastry chefs create stunning dresses, gowns and menswear using chocolate.

My first experience of attending and exhibiting at a chocolate festival was in London at Chocolate Unwrapped, which was owned and organised by my best friend Kate Johns, who is also the owner of Nudge PR. Chocolate Unwrapped was a special place for everyone who loved fine chocolate, and everyone who *wanted* to love fine chocolate. We all shared so much with each other at Kate's chocolate festivals, as they featured chocolate of all types and styles, and demonstrated how this wonderful food satisfies all of our cravings, showing that our attachment to chocolate is stronger than ever before. Kate later became part of the international Salon du Chocolat team, launching a bigger show that featured more exhibitors from around the globe than ever before. I asked Kate about her motivation for launching London's first chocolate festival back in 2010 and what it is about chocolate festivals that draws so many people to them. She explains:

I run a food PR agency and, many years ago, was lucky enough to travel to Belgium with one of my clients. It struck me how their appreciation of chocolate was vastly different to our own in the UK: how incredibly important quality was to them, how their chocolate shops sold out of fresh chocolates every day and, most significantly, how many chocolate shops there actually were! I felt that we needed to promote an appreciation for finer chocolate in the UK, to communicate why consumers should pay a fairer price for a bar of chocolate and to show that there's a huge difference between a bar of well-sourced, well-made chocolate and a sugar-filled snack bar. So, I launched Chocolate Week, persuaded a few London chocolate shops to take part, and then grew it into a nationwide awareness week with over 300 events around the country.

I wanted to bring the chocolate industry together in one place and showcase to consumers how many talented chocolatiers and chocolate makers there were in the UK. I started a chocolate show because it's a very efficient way of doing this: you can taste many different types of chocolate all under one roof. But it also gives consumers a unique opportunity to meet the chocolatiers and chocolate makers, the talented people who are working so incredibly hard to produce the chocolate that we eat. It's also an opportunity to experience chocolate in all its forms, from chocolate sculptures to hot chocolate, patisserie, filled chocolates and, of course, bars.

Although there were lots of Chocolate Week events taking place across the country, I felt that there was room for a main hub for the week, and so I launched Chocolate Unwrapped, a boutique chocolate show. The first one was in an amazing venue at Borough Market in London, with lots of exposed brick – it was very cool. After three years of successful events, I partnered with worldwide chocolate show organisers Salon du Chocolat, and we launched The Chocolate Show at Olympia, London, which was a much bigger event. In our time together, we grew the show to an incredible 18,000 visitors.

Chocolate inspires me so much! I love the history of it. One of the best memories I have with Paul on our chocolate journey is our trip to Honduras to visit the cacao plantations. As part of that expedition, we were privileged to visit some ancient Aztec ruins, which really brought to life how the Aztecs consumed chocolate. I'm fascinated by the fact that chocolate has been consumed in various forms for over 3,500 years. I love that, just like wine, the final taste of the chocolate is impacted by where and how the cacao beans are grown, and I love the many different flavour profiles that chocolate has. Most of all, I love that you can put it into a cake and make the most delicious food on earth!

We also created Choc Tales, an event involving five different rooms with five different cocktails, five chocolatiers and five matching chocolates in an amazing Georgian townhouse in Soho, London. It was a great event, very experiential. I also helped set up the Academy of Chocolate Awards and the International Chocolate Awards. As mentioned, I co-organised the Chocolate Show, which we held at Olympia for four years. As part of the last Chocolate Show in 2017, we created a fantastic exhibition called Choco L'art, where we asked chocolatiers to recreate famous pieces of art in chocolate. As well as just loving the name Choco L'art, I was bowled over by the talent of the chocolatiers, who recreated incredible replicas of artwork from Van Gogh, Da Vinci, Picasso and more.

I love Kate's passion for all things chocolate, and she realised that all of you love it, too, which inspired her to build a successful business. All chocolate shows and festivals, whether consumer or trade, give cacao growers, chocolate makers and chocolatiers a wonderful platform to show off and share their expertise and skills. If you have never visited one, then next time you see an advert for one close to you (or not, if you fancy a road trip adventure), just go, as they always have new and exclusive products created just for that show that you may not get anywhere else again. These chocolate festivals also give you the opportunity to connect with the wonderful people that make all our chocolate possible, from cacao growers to chocolatiers. You may even have the opportunity to taste beans fresh from the pod, or sample freshly roasted beans or cacao liquor. It's such a joyous experience, so don't be shy: lean in and get chatting to these very special people.

Personal and family traditions

Rituals don't have to be steeped in a few thousand years of history to be special and poignant. We all have our own ways of ritualising chocolate, we just don't necessarily see them as rituals. I guess the right term nowadays is probably 'tradition'. If you take a moment to think about this, I know you will all have a chocolate-based tradition or ritual that is unique to you, your friends and family. While you think about your rituals, here are a couple of my own.

When I visit my parents we really are focused on enjoying food: nothing complicated, just the simple, wholesome food we absolutely love to eat. Fish and chips fried in lard or dripping, as they are traditionally prepared in the northeast of England; fresh scones with butter and jam; my mum's brack, a tea loaf that gets better with age, becoming sticky and super-moist. But back to our ritual: after we have enjoyed all of these fantastic foods at dinner time, no matter how full we are, two large black boxes with magnetic lids come out on to the coffee table. They are always a joy and quite impressive: one has chocolate bars in it, a mixture of inclusions, blends and single origins; the other box is packed with all our favourite nostalgic chocolates from Quality Street®, Celebrations and Cadbury Roses. If I'm really lucky and fish around, there may even be some individually wrapped Dairy Milk squares, which never fail to catapult me back to my childhood. It still smells and tastes the same as it always did, and although it's not fine chocolate, it's just as special. We then sit and talk, possibly with a glass of single malt whisky (my stepdad Kevin loves chocolate and whisky together, as do I). This ritual is really important to us. It makes us all smile, it's always a treat and mum still loves to sculpt a tiny foil goblet or wine glass from the foil wrappers (although, annoyingly, many of these are now being replaced with plastic wrappers). Do we count how many chocolates we are eating? Erm … possibly. Does anyone judge or care? Not one bit. This is our special tradition, and we all look forward to it every time we are together. Chocolate is so important in my family that we can enjoy fine cacao chocolate and mainstream confectionery bars equally.

My other ritual is more personal and just for me; it's not something I do with anyone else. It's really quite a mindful, in-the-moment practice that allows me to always remember how incredibly special all chocolate is (or, actually, anything that contains a cacao bean). I carry chocolate with me most of the time. It's like carrying a healing crystal or something special that brings you joy or luck, or just makes you feel attached to the right now. When I carry a wonderful single-origin or blended bar of fine chocolate, I can literally hear it calling my name while it's in my bag: *I'm here, I'm here, I'm yours, I'm good, eat me.* Stay with me on this one, as I really believe that when you carry something with you that you have a connection with, no matter what it is, then it's going to call to you. The chocolate I carry is for my moments when I need escapism and thought. I like really beany chocolate – by this, I mean I like chocolate that tastes the way the beans smell when they are dried and roasted. This means no vanilla, just cane sugar added, really pure and simple in form, but highly complex in flavour.

I'm not shy about saying that I find many parts of life quite stressful, and I use many different ways to manage these difficult moments. If you, like me, find you have these moments in your daily life when you feel a strong need to just be with yourself, then try this ritual. First of all, sit – you could be on the tube, the bus, in the park or a forest, anywhere at all, even at your work desk. Take out the chocolate – a chocolate you have chosen with care and consideration, in the knowledge that it is going to help you feel less stressed. Open it, smell it and eat it however you like. Let it melt in the mouth or chew it. The only thing you are going to think about is the chocolate itself: its texture and taste, and how it makes you feel. It's like a meditation. Do this for as long as you like. By just focusing on this one thing, you give yourself and your brain time to rest, heal and be still, even if only for a few minutes, and you get to enjoy a wonderful flavour experience at the same time. It's a simple ritual, not to be over-thought, not to be formalised, and it's only for you and your inner self. Try it; it's pretty wonderful, and in the process you are feeding your brain with all the beneficial and uplifting chemicals dark chocolate has hidden within it, releasing dopamine to make you feel lighter and ready for the rest of your day.

I've yet to visit all the chocolate festivals I want to, especially those in the growing countries where old traditions are still celebrated, where you have beans straight from the trees and where the history of cacao is ingrained in the culture and heritage of the area. Like Vianne and Anouk in *Chocolat*, I will see where the wind takes me, which new growing countries I will visit next. Until then, I will wait in anticipation of the new stories I've yet to be told, rituals I've yet to experience and festivals I have yet to visit.

Did you know?
The Maya and Aztec rituals around cacao both contain a connection between cacao and blood, and mixing the two was significant. The Maya's spiritual connection to cacao gave them the belief that humans are partially made of chocolate, while the Aztec rituals included giving a slave a mixture of blood and cacao before they were sacrificed as a gift to the gods.

FESTIVALS, RITUALS AND CELEBRATIONS

The 21 very best chocolate recipes

How amazing would it be to have 21 of the very best chocolate recipes in one place for you to make at home? Well, now you do. All are totally indulgent and colourful, and recipes you will want to share with all your family and friends.

I'm not going to suggest that you have to search for single origin or fine chocolate for all of these recipes, but do use chocolate that you love the taste of. You should also make sure that it is real chocolate – so containing no vegetable fats or other nasties.

Have fun with my recipes and never be afraid to add your own colourful finishes, flourishes and flavours.

The recipes

Chocolate mousse
(page 156) It's rich but light, and altogether too good to share.

Chocolate cake
(page 158) The only chocolate cake you will ever need, for every cake occasion.

Hazelnut chocolate spread
(page 161) You know the one. Now you can make it at home, but even better.

Chocolate fudge
(page 162) It's gift time! Make it, eat it, share it.

Dark chocolate truffles
(page 164) Easy, easy, easy, and every chocolate lover's go-to treat.

Triple-chocolate sandwich cookies
(page 166) Best eaten warm.

Hot chocolate
(page 169) Rich and comforting, and perfect for when all you need is a huge hug in a mug.

Chocolate cheesecake
(page 172) A no-bake, super-creamy treat ideal for family lunches.

Chocolate-filled and half-dipped doughnuts
(page 175) Treat day for everyone; over-filled and dipped in chocolate ganache.

Pot au chocolat
(page 178) A classic, simple dessert for when you don't know what to make.

Chocolate truffle torte
(page 180) Want a super-fast and intense chocolate dessert? Then stop right here.

Triple-chocolate babka

(page 182) Bread and chocolate swirled and baked together. You need this in your life.

Chocolate milk

(page 185) Made with real chocolate, this is about to become a staple in your fridge.

Dark chocolate brownie

(page 186) Never dry, never crunchy and always fudgy; try not to eat them all at once.

Chocolate blondie

(page 190) Bright and fun, a creamy cookie dough-style blondie.

Chocolate sandwich

(page 192) Brioche and chocolate, what's not to like? It's over the top and entirely necessary.

100 per cent dark chocolate sugar-free vegan truffles

(page 194) – Yes, they are incredible, intense, and contain no refined sugars.

Dark chocolate martini

(page 196) The real-deal chocolate martini; no chocolate flavouring here.

Chocolate fondant

(page 198) A classic molten chocolate-filled dessert that never fails to impress.

No-churn chocolate ice cream

(page 200) A super-chocolatey chocolate ice cream.

Chocolate tart

(page 202) Impress at every dinner party with this bling and pimped-up dessert.

Chocolate mousse

I hunt out epic chocolate mousse on menus in cafés and restaurants wherever I visit, as a fantastic chocolate mousse is so sublime and joyous that not much else comes close. No frills here: a chocolate mousse doesn't need diamonds and pearls to dress it up, and especially not a whipped cream swirl. What's the point? It adds nothing at all to flavour or appearance. A grating of chocolate or dusting of cocoa powder is all the very best chocolate mousse needs. Always set your mousse in the fridge, but eat it as close to room temperature as possible. Don't expect your homemade mousse to be like those supermarket-bought mass-market chocolate mousses, that really are mostly air. Yours will have lots of air bubbles, but it will also have the structure and density that using a good amount of chocolate gives.

Begin by melting the chocolate and butter together in a heatproof bowl set over a pan of very hot water. Stir in the salt, then add in the egg yolks and mix well. Take off the heat.

In a separate bowl, whisk the whipping cream until stiff and fluffy and add it to the chocolate mixture.

In a clean bowl, whisk the egg whites to stiff peaks, then stir in the sugar and whisk again until stiff and glossy.

Fold the egg whites into the chocolate mixture in two batches. Do not over-mix, but do be sure that there are no unmixed egg whites visible in the mousse.

Carefully scrape the mousse into a serving dish and refrigerate for 1 hour.

Grate over some very dark chocolate, then allow the mousse to sit at room temperature for 15 minutes before serving.

To add even more joy Do nothing! There is enough joy in this mousse already. Just make it often – and share it. This is one of those desserts that is better shared.

Serves 4

200g (7oz) dark chocolate (75 per cent cocoa solids), choose something with a robust flavour, nothing too acidic

75g (2¾oz) unsalted butter

½ teaspoon sea salt flakes, crushed

3 medium free-range eggs, separated

50ml (2fl oz) whipping cream

30g (1oz) unrefined golden caster sugar

grated dark chocolate (at least 85 per cent cocoa solids), to serve

Chocolate cake

This one chocolate cake recipe really does it all, and I'm sharing it with you so you can feel and share the joy of a deep, rich chocolate cake that's light yet supple enough for stacking. It's moist and dessert-like, so also makes a perfect gateau. It will become the only chocolate cake recipe you need.

This is a deep cake, so you can bake it in three one-layer cake tins, or like I do, you can bake it in a deep cake tin with a loose bottom, and then slice it into layers for filling. The cake batter is very wet and liquid, so the baking time is long, and that skewer must come out clean before you remove it from the oven. It's the chocolate cake of all chocolate cakes: deep, generous and unapologetic. I am in love with it, and I hope you fall in love with it too. For my secret buttercream recipe, take a look at page 188.

To make the cake

Preheat the oven to 180°C/160°C fan/350°F/gas 4 and line a 20cm (8in) deep springform cake tin or three shallow (5cm/2in deep) 20cm (8in) cake tins with baking paper.

In the bowl of a stand mixer, mix together the flour, sugars, cocoa powder and baking powder. Add the butter and rub it in by hand, or use the paddle attachment to mix until a breadcrumb-like texture is formed.

In a separate bowl, whisk together the eggs, water, evaporated milk, yogurt, vanilla extract and sea salt.

Add this mixture to the dry ingredients in the stand mixer and whisk for 2 minutes on high speed.

Add the batter to the tin (or tins). Use up all the batter; the tins will be quite full, as we want a very generous height. Now bake: if you're baking in one big tin, it will take up to 1 hour 20 minutes, while shallow tins will take approximately 35 minutes each. Always use the skewer test; if it comes out clean, then the cake is ready.

Allow the cake(s) to sit in the tin(s) for 5 minutes before removing. Peel off the lining paper and leave to cool fully.

Recipe continues overleaf

Serves 12

370g (13oz) self-raising flour

300g (10½oz) unrefined golden caster sugar

150g (5oz) unrefined light muscovado sugar

140g (5oz) cocoa powder

1 teaspoon baking powder

225g (8oz) unsalted butter, cubed

4 medium free-range eggs

285ml (9½fl oz) warm water

200ml (7fl oz) evaporated milk

80ml (2¾oz) natural yogurt

2 teaspoons vanilla extract

1 teaspoon sea salt

For building the cake

1 batch of my secret Sea salted caramel chocolate buttercream

If you're using one big cake, wrap it in a slightly dampened tea towel and refrigerate for 2 hours. This is to help firm the cake up so when you slice the layers, there is less chance of breakages and crumbs.

To build your cake

If you've baked one large cake, remove it from the fridge and slice off the top to level it off (you can nibble on the offcuts). Now slice through the cake to create three layers.

Stick the base cake on to a cake board or plate with a little of the buttercream.

Spread each layer of cake with a generous amount of the buttercream and place them in the refrigerator to set for 30 minutes. Doing this means that when you stack them, the icing stays in the cake instead of splurging out.

Now carefully stack the cakes on top of each other and spread a thin layer of the buttercream over the sides and top of the cake. Refrigerate for 30 minutes.

Finally, spread the remaining buttercream all over the top and sides of the cake; use it all, and do not worry about perfectly smooth sides. Perfection doesn't exist. Just make it as luxurious as you can. For you, this may be swirls, spirals or piping – or, indeed, super-flat tops and sides. Return to the fridge for 1 hour for the icing to firm up.

If you have baked your cakes in shallow separate tins, then follow the instructions above, but without slicing through your cakes to form your layers. You may just need to trim the top of each cake slightly to level off so the cake sits evenly once filled and decorated.

Once decorated (see below), serve at room temperature and never from the fridge. Eat your cake within 1 week of making it, and store in a large airtight container.

∾ To add even more joy

Here we go – and where do we stop?! You can be as bold and daring as you like. Layer up with berries and soft fruits; drizzle some liqueur on the cake before sandwiching together; add fudge pieces between the layers, or chopped toasted nuts; or smother the whole thing in salted caramel so it pours down the sides. What will you do to make this a truly show-stopping chocolate cake?

Decoration

This is totally your call, and I'm up for anything, so take pictures and share so I can see how wonderfully you create your own style of cake.

My favourite chocolate cake decoration is quite simple, yet incredibly striking. I melt dark, milk and white chocolate in separate bowls and allow the chocolate to cool slightly before spreading it on to baking paper or acetate sheets in random dramatic shapes. I chill the sheets, then remove the shapes and attach them to the cake at all angles for a striking finish.

Hazelnut chocolate spread

So many of us have happy childhood memories of hazelnut and chocolate spread, with its iconic sweet taste and velvety texture. Commercially made versions are predominantly made with palm oil and lots of sugar, so making your own means you can switch those out and create a chocolate spread that's full of the good stuff. It's not going to be as smooth as the commercial kind, but it's infinitely more indulgent and nuttier.

Preheat the oven to 170°C/150°C fan/340°F/gas 3½. Spread out the hazelnuts on a baking tray and roast for 10 minutes.

Meanwhile, melt the chocolate in a heatproof bowl set over a pan of hot water.

Once the hazelnuts are roasted, and while still hot, tip them into a blender and begin to blend with the oil. Add the icing sugar and keep blending. When it's as smooth as you can get it, add the cocoa powder, melted chocolate, vanilla extract and sea salt.

Scrape the mixture into a sterilised jar for later, or immediately smother some over a thick slice of white bread.

This will keep at room temperature for up to 2 weeks.

Makes one 250ml (9fl oz) jar

225g (8oz) hazelnuts
40g (1½oz) dark chocolate
(60 per cent cocoa solids)
2 tablespoons vegetable
or hazelnut oil
125g (4½oz) icing sugar
40g (1½oz) cocoa powder
1 teaspoon vanilla extract
1 teaspoon sea salt

Chocolate fudge

It's giveaway time! Sharing, gifting and making batches of sweets for sharing has always been popular, and fudge never loses its appeal. A bubbling mass of butter, sugar and condensed milk will fill your entire house with a sweet, heady aroma, and I can say with authority that although one batch won't last long (because it will be eaten), this fudge does keep for ages, so make lots, bag some up, share it out, and bring some joy to people you know and those you are yet to know. There are two very different types of fudge texture: the type where your teeth sink into density and smoothness, and the more crystalline tablet-style fudge, which has slightly crumbly edges and a softish middle to it. That's my favourite.

Line a 20cm (8in) square baking tray with baking paper.

In a large, heavy-bottomed saucepan, combine the butter, sugar, sea salt, milk and condensed milk over a low heat so that everything slowly melts together.

Increase the heat slightly and allow it to simmer, stirring all the time to prevent it from burning, until it reaches your desired temperature on a digital or sugar thermometer. The higher the temperature, the firmer your fudge will be. So, for a soft fudge, you want to reach 112°C (234°F), while for a firmer fudge, you want 114°C (237°F).

Once you reach your desired temperature, take off the heat and allow the fudge to settle until it has stopped bubbling. Now add the chopped chocolate and mix well until melted. As the fudge cools, it will thicken and crystallise, so keep beating with a wooden spoon until you have a thick paste. Tip this into the prepared baking tray and smooth it out. Allow to cool and set for 4 hours.

Once it's fully set, use a sharp knife to cut it into perfect squares, triangles or fingers, or you can even crumble it up to use on (and in) cakes or on ice cream.

To add more joy You can add so many things to fudge, and the best stage at which to do this is when the fudge has cooled a little and has started to thicken, so go for it and add all your favourite things. I love to add toasted hazelnuts, chopped cookies and candied orange. You can even dip your finished fudge in chocolate, giving you a crisp outer chocolate shell with the gorgeous fudge beneath.

Makes approximately 80 squares of fudge

110g (3¾oz) unsalted butter
425g (15oz) demerara sugar
125ml (4fl oz) whole milk
350ml (12fl oz) sweetened condensed milk
2 teaspoons sea salt flakes, well crushed
150g (5oz) dark chocolate (90–100 per cent cocoa solids), chopped

Dark chocolate truffles

A good chocolate truffle will be the love of your life, the go-to feel-good, taste-good, handmade chocolate that always delivers exactly what has been promised. If these truffles could talk, they would say: *I'm a very sexy chocolate, I'm here to seduce you, and once you have a taste of me, our love affair can never be broken.* That's what I think, anyway, but only when the truffle is super-smooth and super-indulgent. Getting this right can be difficult, but my recipe shows you how. Plus, it's pretty easy to make and so satisfying to eat. Make more than you think you'll need – you know why! They do not need to be neat, perfect balls (unless you want them to be). Just make them the size you want them, with a rippled chocolate casing and coated in a velvety dusting of cocoa powder. Eat at room temperature for the most joyous chocolate experience.

To make the ganache

Mix together the cream, milk, sugar and sea salt in a saucepan over a medium heat. Bring to the boil, then immediately turn off the heat. Take care not to let it boil over.

Place the chopped chocolate in a mixing bowl and pour over half of the hot cream. Mix very well with a whisk, but do not whip air into the ganache. Once smooth, add the remaining cream and mix until you have a glossy emulsion.

Allow to cool to room temperature, then refrigerate for 1 hour.

To coat your truffles

Line a plate or tray with baking paper.

When you're ready, scoop out pieces of ganache to your chosen truffle size. You can either leave them au naturel or roll them into perfect balls with your hands.

Scatter the cocoa powder across a roasting tray or high-sided baking tray.

Using your hands, coat each piece of ganache in the tempered dark chocolate, making sure each one is fully coated, then plunge into the cocoa powder to coat. You may find it easier to have a helper for this stage, to make sure they get coated before the chocolate sets.

Makes up to 100 truffles

For the ganache

150ml (5fl oz) double cream

100ml (3½fl oz) whole milk

50g (1¾oz) unrefined light muscovado sugar

½ teaspoon crushed sea salt flakes

285g (10oz) fine-quality dark chocolate (at least 70 per cent cocoa solids), finely chopped

For the coating

300g (10½oz) cocoa powder

400g (14oz) fine-quality dark chocolate (at least 70 per cent cocoa solids), tempered according to the instructions on pages 63 or 84

As they set in the cocoa powder, remove them and place on the prepared plate or tray to fully set.

Once set, place the truffles in a sieve and gently shake to release any excess cocoa powder.

Taste one, or two or even three. Can you stop?

Store at room temperature and eat within 5 days of making.

To add even more joy These truffles are already so wonderfully indulgent; however, there is always room for a little more joy. Here are a few of my favourite variations for you to try.

- Replace the milk with your favourite tipple, but do not boil your alcohol with the cream. Instead, stir it into the cream ganache once it's smooth so the alcohol doesn't burn off. My top three tipples to add are Irish cream liqueur, single malt whisky and Jamaican rum.
- For something unusual but very decadent try this for Christmas: replace 100ml (3½fl oz) milk with 50g (1¾oz) Stilton or blue cheese. Cook this into the cream, then once the ganache is smooth and mixed, stir in 50ml (2fl oz) port for a stunning port and stilton truffle.

Did you know?
Although they don't contain any real truffle, chocolate truffles are named for their resemblance to the edible fungi.

Triple-chocolate sandwich cookies

I am in the group of people that MUST have a large glass of whole milk whenever I eat cookies. I love the dunk, I love the way the creamy milk seeps into the cookie and slightly softens it. Having said that, this soft cookie needs no dunking – but I still need the milk to enjoy it. I'm using three types of chocolate: a very intense and robust 72 per cent dark chocolate; a smooth and sweet 40 per cent milk chocolate; and a real white chocolate. (Remember: check that the only fat in your white chocolate is cocoa butter, this is what makes it real white chocolate.) You are going to love these, so have your cookie jar at the ready. And it had better be a big one, as you will be making these over and over.

To make the cookies

Preheat the oven to 180°C/160°C fan/350°F/gas 4 and line a baking tray with baking paper.

Melt the butter in a saucepan over a low heat and cook for about 15 minutes until it browns and smells nutty. Take off the heat and let cool for 10 minutes.

In a large bowl, mix together the sugars, flours, sea salt and bicarbonate of soda and mix well, then stir in the eggs, vanilla extract and cooled butter and mix to form a soft dough.

Add all of the chocolate chunks and mix well, then divide the dough into 24 even balls.

Place six balls of dough on the prepared baking tray and bake for 14 minutes exactly.

Remove from your oven and slide off the tray, still on the paper, and leave to cool. Re-line the tray and repeat until all the cookies are baked.

Recipe and ingredients continue overleaf

Makes 12 sandwich cookies

For the cookies

230g (8¼oz) unsalted butter

200g (7oz) unrefined golden caster sugar

230g (8¼oz) unrefined light muscovado sugar

200g (7oz) plain flour

110g (3¾oz) rye flour

2 teaspoons sea salt flakes

1 teaspoon bicarbonate of soda

2 medium free-range eggs

2 teaspoons vanilla extract

150g (5oz) dark chocolate (72 per cent cocoa solids), chopped

150g (5oz) milk chocolate (40 per cent cocoa solids), chopped

150g (5oz) white chocolate, chopped

To sandwich the cookies

In three separate bowls set over pans of hot water, melt half of each of the three types of chocolate for the filling, then take off the heat and add the other half of each type of chocolate and stir to combine and melt. Allow the chocolate to sit for 10 minutes.

Lay 12 cookies, bottom-side up, on a baking tray. Carefully spoon one blob of each kind of chocolate on to the cookie, keeping the blobs separate. Allow to nearly set, then, when it looks fudgy but not runny, place another cookie on top, bottom-side down, to sandwich together, pressing so it sticks.

Allow the cookies to fully set for 30 minutes before enjoying with a huge glass of whole milk. Store in a cookie jar or tin – and share them carefully.

To add more joy Adding extra crunch to cookies is a joy, so toast some almonds or hazelnuts, chop them into pieces and mix them into the dough.

For a festive version, add ground cinnamon, cloves and ginger to the mix, to make them super-cheery and warming.

For sandwiching
200g (7oz) white chocolate
200g (7oz) milk chocolate
(40 per cent cocoa solids)
200g (7oz) dark chocolate
(70 per cent cocoa solids)

Did you know?
During the 19th century some chocolate makers in England were found to be adding red ochre, red lead or brick dust to their chocolate to improve the colour.

Hot chocolate

My strong – or should I say, passionate – views around hot chocolate are well known within my friendship and industry circles. If something is calling itself a hot chocolate, I believe it should always contain actual chocolate, and not just cocoa powder. Adding dark chocolate adds depth and richness, as well as the one thing we all buy a hot chocolate for: comfort. Having fun with hot chocolate is important, whether that means piling it high with toasted marshmallows or stacking in a handful of chocolate shards (page 112). Both are only going to make for a crazy, indulgent, happy time.

Hot chocolate has evolved and changed over hundreds of years, and at times this evolution has stripped out the happiness of what hot chocolate should really be. Say no to milky, weak sachets of instant powder; say no to chocolate-flavoured syrups; and show the door to lacklustre, watery hot chocolate. Hot chocolate should bring a smile to your soul, heart and face, and that's before you even taste it. This is my best hot chocolate recipe. I hope it will make you smile as it does me, and that you will want to make it for everyone you know. It's smooth, rich and indulgent, and brings a warming joy to every particle of your being. Oh, and it has the most amazing sweet cocoa cream to float on top.

Makes 2 generous mugs

For the cocoa cream
15g (½oz) demerara sugar
10g (¼oz) cocoa powder
100ml (3½fl oz) double or
   whipping cream

For the hot chocolate
250ml (9fl oz) whole milk
200ml (7fl oz) double cream
50g (1¾oz) demerara sugar
15g (½oz) cocoa powder
½ teaspoon sea salt
200g (7oz) dark chocolate
   (70 per cent cocoa solids),
   chopped into small pieces

To make the cocoa cream

In a mixing bowl, combine the sugar, cocoa powder and cream and allow to sit for 15 minutes.

Now whisk until velvety soft and light, then set aside for later.

To make the hot chocolate

Combine the milk, cream, sugar, cocoa powder and sea salt in a saucepan over a medium heat until the sugar has dissolved.

Increase the heat to high and stir constantly until very hot but not boiling.

Put the chopped chocolate in a heatproof bowl or large jug, then pour the hot milk mixture over the top and whisk until super-smooth. If you have a hand blender, then I do recommend using it, as this will give a much smoother texture.

Recipe continues overleaf

THE 21 VERY BEST CHOCOLATE RECIPES

You should have a good amount of froth on the surface, so serve your hot chocolate immediately with the froth on top.

Spoon on a generous amount of sweet cocoa cream to finish, and let time stand still as it's just you and the best hot chocolate you've ever had.

∾ To add more joy To add even more joy to your hot chocolate, try adding a measure of cream liqueur, whisky or cognac just before drinking.

Add a grating of nutmeg or use a cinnamon stick to stir flavour into your hot chocolate.

Pile on pillows of whipped cream until it overflows; you know you want to.

Add orange zest for a classic chocolate–orange flavour.

Top your hot chocolate with shavings of your favourite chocolate, or a massive marshmallow.

My all-time favourite addition, though, is a shot of espresso, to make the most awesome mocha you will ever drink.

Did you know?
Until 1847, chocolate was enjoyed only in liquid form at chocolate houses, or at home if you were of wealthy means. It wasn't until Fry & Sons combined cocoa butter with sugar and cocoa mass that the first solid chocolate bar became available.

Chocolate cheesecake

Cheesecake: what a wonderful invention. It's the perfect combination of smooth, creamy and crunchy – and then there are all the delicious toppings. In my opinion, it's one of only a few desserts that is low effort for absolutely maximum impact, and that's before you get super-creative and add those inclusions, sauces and decorations. Chocolate cheesecake needs to be sweet, creamy and slightly salty to help the chocolate flavours really shine. I'm using milk chocolate here. For the filling, choose a higher-percentage milk chocolate with 40–60 per cent cocoa solids, as this will have a much fuller flavour. I like a really deep base and a deep cheesecake filling, so this recipe needs a high-sided tin, but if you like a less deep-filled cheesecake, just halve the filling recipe.

To make the base

Line the base of a 20cm (8in) springform cake tin with baking paper.

Melt the chocolate in a heatproof bowl set over a pan of hot water. Once melted, remove from the heat and stir in the melted butter and crushed cookies.

Press the cookie mixture into the bottom of the tin, letting it come slightly up the sides.

To make the filling

Melt the chocolate in a heatproof bowl set over a pan of hot water. Once melted, take off the heat and let cool to room temperature.

In a bowl, whisk together the cream cheese, cream and icing sugar until thick and glossy.

Add the melted milk chocolate and fold through until fully combined.

Spoon the mixture on to the biscuit base and smooth out. Refrigerate for 2 hours.

Recipe and ingredients continue overleaf

Serves 8 generously

For the base
50g (1¾oz) milk chocolate

75g (2¾oz) unsalted butter, melted

200g (7oz) chocolate chip cookies or chocolate digestives, crushed until sandy

For the filling
150g (5oz) milk chocolate (40–60 per cent cocoa solids)

500g (1lb 2oz) full-fat cream cheese, at room temperature

250ml (9fl oz) double cream, at room temperature

100g (3½oz) icing sugar

To make the chocolate top

Melt the two chocolates together in a bowl set over a pan of very hot water. Take off the heat, then add the butter cubes and salt and mix until glossy.

Remove the cheesecake from the fridge and spread the mixture over the top. Leave to set for 30 minutes at room temperature.

Grate over some dark chocolate, then serve in generous wedges.

ﾍﾞ **To add more joy** Well, this is where you can really go to town and add anything you like to the base or the filling! I love Irish cream liqueur in a cheesecake, so adding a glug to the filling mixture is wonderful, but feel free to include toasted nuts, brownie pieces and sweet spices like ground nutmeg and cinnamon. You could also drizzle lots of caramel on top.

For the chocolate top

125g (4½oz) dark chocolate (60 per cent cocoa solids), plus extra grated, to serve
50g (1¾oz) milk chocolate (40 per cent cocoa solids)
140g (5oz) unsalted butter, chopped into cubes
½ teaspoon crushed sea salt flakes

Did you know?
The first chocolate Easter eggs were developed in France and Germany during the 19th century. These first iterations were solid, however – the first hollow egg was produced by British chocolatiers Fry & Sons in 1873.

Chocolate-filled and half-dipped doughnuts

So many cultures around the world have a variety of fried sweet dough, and I love every one I've ever tried – and why wouldn't I? Some have been dredged in so much icing sugar it made me cough as I tried to take a bite; some are soaked in honey syrup until every fluffy light air bubble in the dough was flooded; and some are filled – and over-filled – with creams and custards. What's not to like? I love a good doughnut, and I'm no snob about it. I enjoy sourdough or baked doughnuts, but give me a soft, fluffy light-yeasted dough, deep-fried, over-filled and dipped in glaze any day. Here is my favourite way of making them. I do not apologise for how wonderfully filthy these are. I'm not a fan of chocolate custard, so I've chosen a soft ganache for the filling, and instead of a glaze, I half-dip my doughnuts chocolate so they stand proud, with a crisp chocolate topping on a super-soft dough and filling.

To make the ganache filling

We will make the filling first, so it's ready for later.

Combine the double cream and sugar in a saucepan over a medium heat. Bring to the boil, then take off the heat.

Place the chopped chocolate in a heatproof bowl and pour the hot cream over the top. Mix well to form a smooth, glossy emulsion and set aside for later.

To make the dough

In a small bowl, combine the yeast and warm water with ½ teaspoon caster sugar. Mix well and set aside for 10 minutes until really frothy.

Once frothy, add all the remaining doughnut ingredients and the yeast mixture to a stand mixer with a dough hook attachment. Mix until a tight dough is formed. This will take up to 10 minutes.

Using your hands, shape the dough into a smooth ball and place in an oiled mixing bowl. Oil the top of the dough, too, as this prevents it drying out, then cover with a damp tea towel. Place somewhere warm for 30–45 minutes until the dough doubles in size.

Recipe and ingredients continue overleaf

Makes 10–12 doughnuts

For the ganache filling
100ml (3½fl oz) double cream
50g (1¾oz) unrefined light
　　muscovado sugar
85g (3oz) dark chocolate
　　(70 per cent cocoa solids),
　　chopped

For the doughnuts
2½ teaspoons fast-action dried
　　yeast
2 tablespoons warm water
2 tablespoons unrefined golden
　　caster sugar, plus ½ teaspoon
　　for the yeast mixture
410g (14½oz) plain flour
235ml (8fl oz) whole milk
55g (2oz) unsalted butter,
　　at room temperature
3 free-range egg yolks

To shape and fry

Line a baking tray with baking paper.

Once the dough has doubled in size, knock it back with your fist to deflate it, then roll it out to a thickness of 2.5cm (1in). Use a cutter to cut out rounds: I use one no more than 7.5cm (3in) in diameter, but you could go smaller if you like, to create mini doughnut bites.

Place the doughnuts on the lined baking tray and carefully cut the baking paper around each one, so each doughnut is sitting on its own individual piece of paper. Cover with a tea towel and place somewhere warm for 45 minutes.

When you're ready to deep-fry, pour the oil into your deep-fat fryer or a high-sided frying pan to a depth of 10cm (4in). Place over a medium heat and heat the oil to 175°C (347°F). Carefully lift the first doughnut by its piece of paper and place it in the hot oil, frying it for 2 minutes per side and removing the paper when it floats away from the doughnut. Lift out on to a wire rack set over a plate so any excess oil can drip away. Repeat with the remaining doughnuts, working in batches of up to three, then leave to cool.

To fill the doughnuts

Once fully cold, the doughnuts can be filled. You will need an icing pipe and a doughnut-filling nozzle. Spoon the filling into the piping bag and plunge the nozzle into the side of the first doughnut, aiming for the middle. Squeeze until it starts to over-fill and leak from the doughnut around the nozzle. Continue until all the doughnuts are filled.

To finish

To finish the doughnuts, plunge each one into the tempered milk chocolate, holding them so that the filling hole is facing upwards. Once the chocolate comes halfway up the doughnut, lift it out and shake off any excess before placing on a baking tray lined with baking paper to set.

Pipe some more filling on to the filling hole and sprinkle with the chocolate flakes. Now you can sink your teeth in and enjoy my favourite doughnut of all time. These need to be eaten within 24 hours of making.

For oiling and deep-frying
vegetable oil (I prefer to use rapeseed oil)

For the chocolate topping
600g (1lb 5oz) milk or dark chocolate, tempered according to the instructions on pages 63 or 84

For the decoration
1 bar of white, dark or milk chocolate, roughly grated into large flakes

෴ To add more joy

Be creative with how you fill and decorate your doughnuts, as anything goes: jam-filled, cream-filled, caramel-filled would all be delicious.

Use sprinkles and cacao nibs to decorate the dipped chocolate before it sets.

Doughnut sandwich – if you don't have a piping bag and nozzle, then slice your doughnuts like bagels and sandwich them together with ganache – or ice cream or caramel – and then dip in chocolate.

Pot au chocolat

A pot au chocolat only tastes as good as the chocolate it's made with, so consider your choice of chocolate carefully and taste different varieties before committing to the recipe, looking for a good balance in flavour and finish.

Preheat the oven to 160°C/140°C fan/325°F/gas 3.

Combine the cream, sea salt, sugar and vanilla in a saucepan over a medium heat. Bring to the boil, then immediately turn off the heat. Mix well and allow the vanilla to infuse for 5 minutes.

Place the chopped chocolate in a heatproof bowl.

Bring the cream mixture back to the boil, then pour it over the chocolate. Whisk until glossy – do this by hand, and avoid beating any air into the mix.

In a separate bowl, whisk together the egg yolks until smooth and pale.

Add the hot chocolate cream to the eggs a little at a time and whisk until smooth.

Divide the mixture between your pots and place on a baking tray. Put the tray in the oven, then immediately turn the oven off and leave the pots in the oven in the residual heat until the oven is cold (this can take about 8 hours, depending on your oven, so I usually leave them overnight).

Refrigerate the pots for 1 hour, then allow them to come to room temperature before serving. Top each one with a light dusting of cocoa powder and your favourite decoration; edible flowers add a wonderful pop of colour.

Makes 4 pots

400ml (14fl oz) double cream
pinch of crushed sea salt flakes
75g (2¾oz) unrefined golden caster sugar
1 teaspoon vanilla extract, or ½ vanilla pod, scraped
185g (6½oz) dark chocolate (65–70 per cent cocoa solids), chopped into small pieces
4 medium free-range egg yolks
cocoa powder, for dusting

To add even more joy
Introduce seasonal twists. My favourites are:

For spring, gently poach some rhubarb with ginger and place in the bottom of the pots.

For summer, place raspberries in the bottom of the pots.

For autumn, put pears poached in red wine in the bottom of the pots.

For winter, add ground cinnamon and orange zest to cream when heating to infuse.

It's your call: be adventurous, or revel in the simplicity.

Chocolate truffle torte

If you are short of time and need to whip up a dessert that's wonderfully chocolatey and impressive, with just a few ingredients, then stop right here. My chocolate torte recipe ticks all the boxes, and it looks like you spent the entire day in the kitchen making it.

The base is a no-bake fudgy almond, white chocolate and honey layer, and the chocolate torte itself calls for just three ingredients. It's a dessert you can always have on standby, and my top tip is to always have an emergency carton of long-life cream in your pantry for occasions when you need to make a dessert in no time at all.

To make the base

Line the base of a 20cm (8in) springform cake tin or loose-based tart tin with a disc of baking paper, and oil the sides.

Melt the white chocolate in a heatproof bowl set over a pan of hot water, then take off the heat. At the same time, gently warm the honey in a small saucepan over a low heat. Add the honey and ground almonds to the chocolate and mix well.

Spoon this mixture into the bottom of your tin and spread it out evenly, pressing it down firmly. Place in the fridge for 30 minutes.

To make the torte filling

Melt the dark chocolate in heatproof bowl over a pan of hot water, then take off the heat and allow to cool for 10 minutes.

In a bowl, sprinkle the sugar over the cream and very carefully mix it in, taking care not to whisk the cream too much: you want the cream to just have soft peaks.

Fold in the melted chocolate and booze, if using, until you have a smooth and chocolatey cream. Spoon this into your tin and smooth the top off with a palette knife. Refrigerate for 30 minutes.

To decorate

Dust the top of the torte with cocoa powder, then scatter over the flaked almonds.

Serves 8

For the base
vegetable oil, for greasing
50g (1¾oz) white chocolate
75g (2¾oz) runny honey
75g (2¾oz) ground almonds

For the filling
250g (9oz) dark chocolate (any percentage you like)
75g (2¾oz) unrefined light muscovado sugar
250ml (9fl oz) double cream, at room temperature
50ml (2fl oz) your favourite spirit or liqueur (optional)

For the decoration
cocoa powder for, dusting
50g (1¾oz) flaked almonds, toasted

To add more joy There is enough joy in this dessert, so I'm not going to suggest anything to you at all. Sometimes simplicity is the best.

Triple-chocolate babka

I need this recipe in my life, and I hope you will adopt it and enjoy it as much and as often as I do. The finished result looks as though the recipe is complicated and tricky, but if you follow the times carefully for proving and baking, you will have no problem creating this totally indulgent and impressive chocolate loaf. Babka was developed in the Jewish communities in the 19th century, using leftover challah dough swirled with fruit jam and sweet spices like cinnamon. And then, because it's so wonderful, it was adopted by bakers across the globe, with many variations emerging, including, of course, chocolate. Feel free to play with using different chocolates in this recipe. You could also add things like chopped nuts, dried fruits and peanut butter. This recipe takes two days, as the dough must rest in the fridge overnight, so make sure you have allocated enough time to make it. I promise you, it's so worth it.

To make the dough (day one)

Ensure all your dough ingredients are at room temperature before you begin.

In a saucepan over a low heat, warm the milk to 110°C (230°F), then take off the heat and mix in the yeast and ½ teaspoon sugar. Leave for 10 minutes until frothy.

In a stand mixer with a dough hook attachment, combine the flour, sugar, salt, eggs and vanilla extract, along with the frothy yeast mixture. Mix until the dough comes away from the sides of the bowl.

Add half of the butter and mix for 5–6 minutes until it has been absorbed by the dough. Now add the remaining butter and mix for 7 minutes until you have a tight, smooth dough. If the dough is too wet, add 1 tablespoon flour and mix well.

Place the dough in a large, clean, oiled bowl and cover with a clean tea towel. Set aside in a warm place for 1½ hours until the dough has risen and doubled in size.

Knock back the dough with your fist, then cover the bowl with clingfilm and refrigerate overnight.

Recipe and ingredients continue overleaf

Makes 2 loaves in large 13 × 20cm (8 × 5in) loaf tins, or 3 in smaller 20 × 8cm (8 × 3in) loaf tins

For the dough

120ml (4fl oz) whole milk

7g fast–action dried yeast

65g (2¼oz) unrefined golden caster sugar, plus ½ teaspoon for the yeast mixture

535g (1lb 3oz) strong white bread flour

1½ teaspoons sea salt

4 large free–range eggs

1 teaspoon vanilla extract

140g (5oz) unsalted butter, at room temperature

vegetable oil, for oiling

To make the filling (day two)

To make the filling, combine the cream, sugar and salt in a saucepan over a medium heat. Bring to a simmer, then take off the heat.

Place the dark chocolate in a heatproof bowl and pour over the warm cream. Mix until smooth and glossy. Add the butter and vanilla extract and mix well until fully combined.

Allow to cool to room temperature before using.

To shape and bake (day two)

Generously butter your loaf tins and line with baking paper. Leave some paper overhanging, as this will help lift the babka out of the tins later.

Now take the dough and divide into two or three equal parts, depending on how many tins you are using.

If making two loaves, roll each piece of dough into a rectangle measuring 20 × 40cm (8 × 16in). If make three smaller loaves, then roll each piece of dough into a rectangle measuring 20 × 30cm (8 × 12in). Divide the chocolate cream filling between the rectangles and spread it out in an even layer, then sprinkle the chopped milk and white chocolate evenly over the top.

Roll each one up like a swiss roll and cut in half lengthways, leaving one end attached as though you are about to plait it, exposing the filling and layers of dough.

Now twist each of the cut babka to make spirals of dough. Spiral and fold these into the tins, then cover again. Leave to prove for 1½ hours at room temperature until they nearly double in size.

Preheat the oven to 175°C/155°C fan/345°F/gas 3½.

Bake your babkas for 45–50 minutes for two larger ones or 30–40 minutes for three smaller ones until cooked through and golden brown. They should sound hollow when tapped.

Allow the babkas to cool in the tins for 15 minutes before turning out to cool fully. Try to resist eating them while they are still very hot.

To glaze, warm the golden syrup over a gentle heat, then brush it over each babka for a super-sticky, glossy shine.

Warm babka is wonderful, so set your timer for 1 hour, then cut and enjoy. Eat your babka as freshly as possible: as with all bread, they will stale after a couple of days.

For the chocolate filling

175ml (6fl oz) double cream

100g (3½oz) unrefined light muscovado sugar

½ teaspoon sea salt

200g (7oz) dark chocolate (70 per cent cocoa solids), chopped

110g (3¾oz) unsalted butter, cubed

2 teaspoons vanilla extract

100g (3½oz) milk chocolate, chopped

100g (3½oz) white chocolate, chopped

For the glaze

50g (1¾oz) golden syrup

To add more joy I love a nutty babka, so add toasted chopped almonds and hazelnuts with the chocolate filling. And this is not authentic at all, but I adore a winter babka, so I add orange zest and ground cinnamon, nutmeg and cardamom to my chocolate filling for a very festive loaf.

Chocolate milk

I will confess I am not a lover of chocolate milk unless I make it myself, as most chocolate milks do not really taste of chocolate and are quite diluted in flavour. My recipe is full-flavoured, and you can sweeten it to your liking by increasing or reducing the sugar. Use a really robust dark chocolate – and that doesn't mean a higher percentage, necessarily, but a chocolate with a really strong cocoa aftertaste and well-rounded flavour, rather than an acidic Madagascan, which won't be pleasant with milk. Once made, remember to shake or mix it well before drinking to ensure that any chocolate that has settled gets distributed through the milk. You will never buy ready-made chocolate milk ever again.

Pour half the milk into a saucepan over a medium heat and bring to the boil.

Put the chopped chocolate in a measuring jug, then pour the hot milk over the top. Add the syrup or honey and the sea salt and blend until smooth. (Do take care when blending very hot liquids: start on a low speed setting and cover the blender and top of the jug with a cloth to avoid splatter and spillage. Pour in the cold milk and blend again.

To serve, pour over ice and enjoy.

This will keep it in the fridge in a jar or bottle for up to a week. Just remember to give it a shake before you drink it, as it will settle and separate slightly. This is normal.

To add even more joy Brace yourself for the ultimate hard chocolate milk – for adults only, of course. This recipe is fantastic with a shot of coconut rum, which immediately turns it into a Caribbean chocolate coconut hardshake. What's not to love?

For the kids, add a generous bunch of chopped mint leaves to the milk when it's in the saucepan, then bring to the boil and strain to remove the leaves before adding the mint-infused milk to the chocolate for a super mint-chocolate milk.

Makes 1 litre (1¾ pints)

400ml (14fl oz) whole milk
100g (3½oz) dark chocolate (65–70 per cent cocoa solids), chopped into small pieces
50ml (2fl oz) maple syrup, agave syrup or runny honey
pinch of sea salt flakes
ice cubes, to serve

Dark chocolate brownie

The brownie is one of the most contested cakes of all time. I once entered a national food competition with the brownie recipe I use for my chocolate business, where it is one of our bestsellers. The judges did not agree, and I was disqualified with the comments, 'This is not a brownie!' I was speechless, and I still lament it to this day.

So, where do you stand with the texture? Soft and fudgy from edge to edge, top to bottom, like me, or crumbly on the outside and soft in the middle? Well, I think both are absolutely OK but I favour the fudgy version rather than cakey. Be creative and add the ingredients you love to the batter: nuts, fruits or spices, they will all just make it even better.

Preheat the oven to 175°C/155°C fan/345°F/gas 3½ and line a 20 × 25cm (8 × 10in) baking tin with baking paper.

In a saucepan over a medium heat, combine the butter, sugars and honey or syrup together until melted and bubbling. Take off the heat and add 325g (11½oz) of the chocolate, mixing well until all the chocolate has melted.

Stir in the vanilla and sea salt, then add the eggs and whisk until smooth and glossy. Add the flour and mix well, then pour the batter into prepared tin and allow to cool.

Once cool, scatter the remaining 200g (7oz) chocolate chunks over the surface of the batter and swirl them into the brownie using a teaspoon.

Bake for 35 minutes, rotating the tray halfway through cooking, then remove from the oven and allow to cool fully in the tin. Refrigerate overnight.

The next day, remove the brownie from the tin and cut off the edges so that everyone gets a middle piece. Then cut into 15 pieces. (Don't throw the edges away, as they can be dipped in chocolate or used in cake pops or desserts.)

Enjoy at room temperature. Store in an airtight container and eat within 2 weeks of making.

Makes 15 brownies

220g (7¾oz) unsalted butter
150g (5oz) unrefined light muscovado sugar
100g (3½oz) unrefined golden caster sugar
115g (4oz) runny honey, agave syrup or maple syrup
525g (1lb 2oz) dark chocolate (60–70 per cent cocoa solids), chopped into chunks
2 teaspoons vanilla extract
1 teaspoon sea salt
5 medium free-range eggs
90g (3¼oz) plain flour

To add more joy When it comes to brownies, for me it's all about nuts, especially pecans and macadamias, with their luxurious oily texture. However, if it's a special occasion, then why not make a dark chocolate ganache and spread it over the cold brownie before cutting to make a seriously indulgent dessert.

Secret bonus joyful recipe: Sea salted caramel chocolate buttercream

While I was writing this book, I had the joy of creating a 40th birthday cake for two very special clients and friends of mine, Alex and Emily Edwards. One thing I always make sure of is that the filling for any cake is as epic and wonderful as the cake itself. I wanted it to be not too sweet, not fatty or overly fluffy, but definitely full of flavour, and it had to be just as deep as the cakes themselves in every layer. So, for the very first time, here is my recipe for the very best chocolate buttercream for all cakes everywhere.

To make the sea salted caramel

Melt the butter, sugar and salt together in a saucepan over a medium heat and simmer for 2 minutes. Take off the heat and stir in the cream, then return to the heat and bring to the boil, still stirring.

Take off the heat and allow to cool fully before using.

To make the buttercream

Make sure all the ingredients are at room temperature before you start. Melt the dark chocolate in a bowl set over a pan of hot water and allow to cool.

In a stand mixer with a paddle attachment, cream the butter until soft, then add half the icing sugar and mix slowly until fully incorporated. Increase the speed up to high and whip for 2 minutes.

Add the rest of the icing sugar, along with the evaporated milk and vanilla. Mix on slow until fully incorporated, then whip on high for 3 minutes.

Now add the cold sea salted caramel and mix through fully. Scrape down the sides of the bowl and mix again.

Add the cool but melted chocolate and whip on high for 30 seconds. The buttercream is now ready to use.

You can make this up to 24 hours in advance; store at room temperature and mix well before using.

Makes enough to fill and coat a 20cm (8in) cake

75g (2¾oz) dark chocolate
250g (9oz) unsalted butter, at room temperature
500g (1lb 2oz) icing sugar
50ml (2fl oz) evaporated milk
4 teaspoons vanilla extract
150g (5oz) sea salted caramel (see below)

For the sea salted caramel

50g (2oz) unsalted butter
50g (2oz) unrefined light muscovado sugar
8g (⅓oz) sea salt flakes
50ml (2fl oz) double cream

Tip Use the leftover salted caramel to spread in the cake with the buttercream.

Chocolate blondie

There has been a huge surge in blondie excitement, and it's all down to it being an excellent vehicle for additional flavours and textures. A blondie on its own is very one dimensional and tastes very sweet, usually with vanilla aftertaste from the white chocolate used. However, the excitement grows when you start adding other things into them pre-baking. All kinds of cookies and chocolate bars can be added, and they make more really fun and often kitsch-looking blondies. If you love sweet things – *very* sweet – then blondies are for you, and my recipe celebrates blondies at their best: fun, super-indulgent, and unapologetically sweet.

Preheat the oven to 180°C/160°C fan/350°F/gas 4 and line a 20cm (8in) square baking tray with baking paper.

Melt the butter, salt and sugar in a saucepan over a medium heat until it begins to simmer.

Remove from the heat and add the white chocolate, whisking well. This mixture will look split and a little odd, but don't worry.

Add the eggs and vanilla extract, mixing well until smooth, then add the flour. Mix very well to combine, and finally stir in the pecans.

Pour the mixture into the prepared tray and level out. Drizzle over the sea salted caramel and swirl into the blondie with a fork. Then scatter with raspberries for some sharpness and colour.

Bake for 25–30 minutes, rotating the tray halfway through cooking. The blondie is ready when it is springy to the touch but still a bit soft.

Allow to cool, then refrigerate overnight.

The next day, remove from the tray and cut the blondies by trimming off the edges so that the cakey edge is removed and all the pieces are fudgy, then cut into 12 pieces. Don't throw the edges away, as they can be dipped in chocolate or used in cake pops or desserts.

Ꮼ **To add more joy** This is your time to shine and add anything you love to the blondie batter: blueberries, nuts, bananas, coconut, orange zest, cookies … Anything goes, so don't hold back. Just get creative and have fun.

Try dipping them in chocolate and adding sprinkles or any other decorations you like to make them really pop.

Makes 12 blondies

200g (7oz) salted butter
¼ teaspoon sea salt flakes, crushed
160g (5¾oz) unrefined golden caster sugar
320g (11¼oz) white chocolate, chopped
3 medium free-range eggs, whisked
1 teaspoon vanilla extract
280g (10oz) plain flour
65g (2¼oz) pecans, chopped
200g (7oz) raspberries
150g (5oz) sea salted caramel (see page 188)

THE 21 VERY BEST CHOCOLATE RECIPES

Chocolate sandwich

All you can do when you say 'chocolate sandwich' is smile – and this sandwich is going to put the biggest smile on your face when you are eating it, and leave you with an even bigger smile in your heart when you have finished. This recipe offers a crunchy, caramelised first bite, then a pillowy soft brioche, before you sink your teeth into slightly salted chocolate butter before finally encountering a slice of unbelievable dark chocolate ganache that is slightly melting and fudgy. It's chocolate porn in its finest form.

To make the ganache filling

Pour the cream into a saucepan over a medium heat. Bring to the boil, then take off the heat.

Place the dark chocolate in a heatproof bowl and pour the hot cream over the top. Whisk until you have a glossy ganache.

Set aside to cool to room temperature.

To make the sweet chocolate butter

Simply cream all the ingredients together in a bowl until smooth.

To build your sandwich

Butter all the brioche slices on one side; this will be the outside surface of the sandwich.

Spread the reverse sides with the sweet chocolate butter, then be lavish and spoon a thick layer of the ganache filling on to two of the brioche slices, leaving a 1cm (½in) gap around the edges.

Top with the other two slices of brioche, with the sweet chocolate butter facing down into the sandwich, and press down.

Generously dust the sandwiches on both sides with icing sugar.

Place a frying pan over a medium heat and add the sandwiches. Fry for 2 minutes on each side, taking care not to burn them.

Remove from the pan, slice diagonally, and enjoy the most luxurious sandwich you have ever eaten.

Makes 2 sandwiches

4 thick slices of brioche
50g (1¾oz) unsalted butter
25g (1oz) icing sugar

For the ganache filling
75ml (2¾fl oz) whipping cream
75g (2¾oz) dark chocolate
    (65–75 per cent cocoa solids),
    chopped

For the sweet chocolate butter
100g (3½oz) unsalted butter,
    at room temperature
25g (1oz) icing sugar
20g (¾oz) cocoa powder
1 teaspoon sea salt flakes,
    crushed

To add more joy Really?! Can we add more joy to an already joy-filled sandwich? Yes, of course we can – and it's so easy. Just slice in a banana or add some peanut butter, a sprinkle of dried chilli flakes, or even some chopped toasted hazelnuts.

100 per cent dark chocolate sugar-free vegan truffles

OK, yes: you read this correctly. Dark chocolate truffles made with 100 per cent cocoa solids and no refined sugars; in fact, they are sweetened with an alternative sugar. They taste absolutely wonderful and are intense, rich and smooth without being too strong. And you won't believe this, but they contain no dairy at all. So what you get is impact and purity without the sugar spike. I just add a touch of olive oil for smoothness, and it adds a peppery flavour, too. Try them once – it won't be your last time.

To make the ganache

Combine the water, sweetener and sea salt in a saucepan over a high heat and bring to a simmer.

Place the chopped chocolate in a heatproof bowl and pour over half of the hot liquid chocolate. Blend with a hand blender to emulsify, then add the rest of the liquid and mix well with the hand blender until glossy.

Add the olive oil and mix in well with the hand blender. Allow the ganache to cool to room temperature, then refrigerate for 1 hour.

To coat

When you're ready to continue, use a teaspoon scoop out 40 pieces of ganache. Scatter the cocoa powder over high-sided tray and toss the truffles through to coat. Allow the truffles to fully set in the cocoa powder for 5 minutes, then shake in a sieve to release any loose cocoa powder.

Allow them to come to room temperature for 10 minutes, then enjoy. They can be kept in the fridge for 5 days in an airtight container.

To add more joy Now things can get interesting, as a water ganache truffle means you can use any liquid that is not dairy. So, here we go: instead of water, use strong tea of different varieties, coffee, orange juice, red wine, champagne, coconut milk or coconut water, fruit juices and purées, craft beer ... I could go on. You could also add herbs to the water to infuse. So get creative and remember to write down all your adapted recipes for future reference.

Makes 40 truffles

For the ganache
200ml (7fl oz) water
75g (2¾oz) stevia or erythritol
½ teaspoon sea salt
2 teaspoons extra virgin olive oil
200g (7oz) dark chocolate (100 per cent cocoa solids), chopped

For dusting
100g (3½oz) cocoa powder

Dark chocolate martini

What makes a wonderfully special lunch or dinner? The atmosphere, champagne, friends, food and music? Well, all of these – and now you can include my real chocolate martini in the mix. A martini is sophisticated, elegant and poised – and lethally intoxicating, so should be drunk with consideration and in moderation (especially with chocolate added, as it can be easy to forget how strong they are). I've experienced some jaw-droppingly terrible chocolate martinis around the world, as so many are made with chocolate-flavoured syrups and rarely real chocolate. Dark chocolate brings a luxe experience to this drink, with so much flavour and smoothness that you will fall in love with this version. All you need to do is remember to have a bar of dark chocolate in the house at all times.

To make the chocolate syrup

Combine the water, syrup and cocoa powder in a saucepan over a high heat. Bring to the boil, then reduce the heat to low and simmer for 2 minutes.

Place the chopped chocolate in a heatproof bowl or jug. Take the water and syrup mixture off the heat and pour it over the chocolate, then whisk well until smooth.

Leave to cool fully. The syrup will keep in a jar in the fridge for up to a month.

To make the perfect chocolate martini

Chill or freeze two martini glasses.

Add 4–6 ice cubes to a cocktail shaker or jam jar, then pour in the gin or vodka, followed by the syrup. Put on the lid and shake well for 30 seconds. Strain into the chilled glasses, with a grating of chocolate or a dusting of cocoa powder on top.

↷ **To add more joy** Add some freshly chopped mint to the shaker for a cool mint–choc martini – or you even add some cold espresso for a mocha moment.

Serves 2

For the chocolate syrup (makes enough for 7 martinis)
250ml (9fl oz) water
75ml (2½fl oz) golden syrup or agave syrup
15g (½oz) cocoa powder
100g (3½oz) dark chocolate (at least 70 per cent cocoa solids), chopped

For the martinis
ice cubes
2 double shots gin or vodka
2 double shots chocolate syrup (see above)
grated dark chocolate or cocoa powder, to serve

Chocolate fondant

The craze of the chocolate fondant is as strong as it has ever been. Why? Because it's so delicious, so moreish and so indulgent. This is happy food in its purest form: a cakey outer shell with a warm molten centre of velvety chocolate. There isn't one thing not to like about a chocolate fondant, and once you try it, this recipe will become your dinner-party staple. Follow the cooking time to the second; if you don't, then you won't get the joy of chocolate lava flowing out. The best bit is, you can make these in advance and cook them when you need them. They can even be made in advance and frozen, however you should always defrost them in the fridge overnight before baking. So fantastic when you have a last-minute dinner guest or an impromptu indulgence moment.

To make the batter

Melt the butter in a saucepan over a medium heat. Once melted, take off the heat and add the chocolate, mixing until smooth and fully melted. Stir in the crushed sea salt.

In a bowl, lightly whisk the eggs and sugar together, then add the chocolate mixture and stir. Finally, add the flour and mix well.

To prepare

Line 4 small pudding basins or dariole moulds by brushing the soft butter across the bases and up the sides, then dusting with cocoa powder. Turn over and tap out any excess.

Divide the batter between the prepared moulds and refrigerate for 1 hour, or cover with clingfilm and bake when needed. You can keep them unbaked in the fridge for 3 days, or freeze for up to a month.

To bake

Preheat your oven to 180°C/160°C fan/350°F/gas 4.

Bake your fondants for 9 minutes, or until the filling is set around the edge yet still slightly wobbly in the centre. Remove from the oven and allow to stand for 1 minute.

To turn out, place a dessert plate on top of the fondant and invert, lifting off the mould. Take care as they are fragile.

Serve immediately. I love to serve these with vanilla ice cream.

Makes 4

For the batter

120g (4oz) unsalted butter
100g (3½oz) dark chocolate (65–75 per cent cocoa solids)
1 teaspoon crushed sea salt flakes
4 medium free-range eggs
100g (3½oz) unrefined golden caster sugar
90g (3¼oz) plain flour

For preparing the moulds

20g (¾oz) unsalted butter, softened
20g (¾oz) cocoa powder

ꝯ To add more joy

The simple things are always the best: grate the zest of 1 orange into the mixture before adding the flour for a chocolate–orange fondant, or add a few drops of peppermint oil for an after-dinner mint fondant.

THE 21 VERY BEST CHOCOLATE RECIPES

No-churn chocolate ice cream

I do not own an ice-cream machine, and I really dislike commercially made chocolate ice cream, as I have yet to find one that actually tastes of chocolate. It's very difficult to get the flavour profile right, as chocolate eaten at such cold temperatures cannot be appreciated fully and many of the beautiful complexities of the cacao bean are lost. Quite often, they're lost to artificial ingredients, with very little actual chocolate being used and far too much sugar. Of course, this was a challenge set: to create a no-churn chocolate ice cream that is silky smooth and has a rich, balanced yet intense dark chocolate flavour. Give this recipe a try, and be creative as you can with other additions: my favourite variation is chopped pecans, sea salt and stem ginger.

Freeze a container for the ice cream for 1 hour before making.

In a bowl, whisk the cream until soft peaks form, then set aside.

Melt the chocolate in a heatproof bowl set over a pan of hot water. Once melted, stir in the condensed milk until smooth and well combined. Add the vanilla extract, then fold in the whipped cream. Finally, fold in the white, milk and dark chocolate chunks.

Transfer the mixture to the freezer container and cover, then freeze for at least 2 hours before scooping.

To add more joy Melt some dark chocolate and generously pour it over the top of the ice cream, leaving it for a few moments so it sets with a crunch.

Pour a warm espresso over a scoop of this ice cream for the perfect affogato.

Best of all, use this ice cream to make the craziest ice cream sundae, with chocolate sauce, brownie chunks, broken cookies, fudge sauce and even more brownie chunks. Just go for it, and have some foodie fun times.

Serves 8 generously

For the ice cream
600ml (20 fl oz) double or whipping cream

100g (3½oz) dark chocolate (at least 80 per cent cocoa solids)

450ml (16fl oz) sweetened condensed milk, at room temperature.

2 teaspoons vanilla extract

For the chocolate chunks
50g (1¾oz) white chocolate, chopped into small chunks

50g (1¾oz) milk chocolate, chopped into small chunks

50g (1¾oz) dark chocolate (at least 70 per cent cocoa solids), chopped into small chunks

Chocolate tart

Proportions are so important when it comes to creating a chocolate tart that exceeds all your expectations. The pastry cannot be too thick or soft; the filling has to be soft and silky, not tough and chewy; and the intensity of chocolate has to be so well balanced that at the end of a meal, you can still enjoy the dessert without being overwhelmed. My recipe addresses all of these, so that it's just what you expect from a glorious chocolate tart. Crisp pastry, soft, silky and well-balanced chocolate filling, and delicate yet architecturally impressive chocolate decorations. You will feel so special eating it and serving it at your next dinner party. Never serve it chilled, as this makes the pastry and the chocolate filling too cold to melt in the mouth. If it's a warm day, though, then keep the decoration in the fridge until just before serving.

To make the sweet pastry case

First, make the sweet pastry: it's super-easy. In a bowl, cream together the butter and sugar until smooth. Add the egg and mix well until smooth, then stir in the salt, flour and cocoa powder to form a smooth paste. Wrap in a sheet of baking paper and chill for 1 hour.

Knead until the paste is pliable, then roll out on a lightly floured worktop to a thickness of 3mm (⅛in). Lift the pastry with the rolling pin and use it to line a greased 20cm (8in) loose-based shallow tart tin, leaving an overlap of pastry around the edge of the tin. Chill for 30 minutes.

Preheat the oven to 175°C/155°C fan/345°F/gas 3½.

Crumple a sheet of baking paper, then flatten it out. Lay it over the pastry and fill to the top with uncooked rice or lentils or baking beans.

Blind-bake the pastry case for 15–20 minutes, then remove the rice or lentils and baking paper and bake again for 10 minutes. The pastry should look dry and crisp. Leave it in the tin to cool.

You can freeze any leftover pastry to use another time.

To make the ganache filling

Melt the dark and milk chocolate together in a heatproof bowl set over a pan of hot water. Once melted, take off the heat.

Recipe and ingredients continue overleaf

Serves 6

For the sweet pastry
125g (4½oz) unsalted butter, at room temperature
85g (3oz) icing sugar
1 medium free-range egg, beaten
½ teaspoon sea salt
200g (7oz) plain flour, plus extra for dusting
1 teaspoon cocoa powder

For the ganache filling
200g (7oz) dark chocolate (66 per cent cocoa solids)
100g (3½oz) milk chocolate
200ml (7fl oz) whipping cream
50g (1¾oz) unrefined light muscovado sugar
½ teaspoon sea salt flakes

Combine the cream, sugar and sea salt in a saucepan over a medium heat. Bring to the boil then take off the heat right away.

Pour the cream mixture into the melted chocolate and whisk until smooth.

Pour the ganache into the tart case, filling it to the very top. Allow to cool at room temperature and refrigerate for 1 hour.

Trim off any excess pastry from the tart edge then carefully lift the tart from the tin.

To decorate

Place the chocolate in a heatproof bowl set over a pan of hot water. This time, melt the chocolate half way, so there are still some solid pieces of chocolate in the bowl among the melted chocolate. Now take it off the heat and keep stirring until all the chocolate has melted. Leave for 15 minutes. then stir again.

Scrunch up 4 pieces of baking paper measuring about 21 × 30cm (8¼ × 11¾in), then smooth them out on your worktop.

Divide the melted chocolate between the sheets and spread it out into a layer about 1mm thick. It doesn't have to reach all the way to the edges, nor does it have to be neat.

Place the chocolate sheets in the fridge, stacked on top of each other, and chill for 30 minutes.

Once chilled, peel off the paper and allow the chocolate to break and splinter.

Push the chocolate shards into the top of the tart so they stand upright. You could begin in the centre and work outwards in concentric circles, or arrange them in a pattern moving from one side to the other.

Using some shimmer powder or edible gold leaf (or even both if you want to go super bling), decorate some of the edges of the chocolate pieces using a small, clean paintbrush.

Enjoy the tart at room temperature.

To add more joy The ganache recipe can be flavoured very easily: add orange zest to the cream for a zingy chocolate–orange tart, or infuse the cream with some sweet herbs, like basil or mint.

For my favourite winter chocolate tart, I replace some of the cream with rum or whisky and sprinkle in a little ground nutmeg or cinnamon.

If you love berries, halve some raspberries and blueberries and line the tart case with them before pouring over the ganache.

For the decoration
300g (10½oz) dark chocolate (66 per cent cocoa solids), chopped
1 teaspoon cocoa powder
gold shimmer powder or edible gold leaf

Index

spikes and spirals 114
Montecuma, Aztec emperor 33
motorbike, chocolate 128
moulds, magnetic chocolate
111
mousse, chocolate 154, 156
Mozart, W.A.
Cosi Fan Tutte 114
music, chocolate in 125–7
'My Spring' sculpture 129–30

N

Nacional beans 17, 58
nibs 24
nipples of Venus 125, 132–4
Nudge PR 148

O

oranges
chocolate-orange death by
chocolate 138–9
Original Beans 58

P

Pacari 33, 58
packaging 81–3
peanuts
peanut caramel bar 87, 91–2
smooshed bar 97
Peralta, Santiago 33
personal rituals 150–1
phenylethylamine 18
Pollard, Art 57
pot au chocolat 154, 179
Psycho (film) 126

R

raisins
Caribbean rum and raisin 88
smooshed bar 97
raw chocolate 33
refrigeration, effects of 41
Roger, Patrick 130
roses, chocolate 115

ruby chocolate 30–1
rum
Caribbean rum and raisin 88
rum chocolate milk 185

S

Salon du Chocolat 147
sandwich, chocolate 155, 192
sauce, chocolate 65
sculptures, chocolate 127–30
sea salted caramel chocolate
buttercream 159, 188
shards 112
shimmer powders 109
shortbread fingers, chocolate
and caramel 93
single-bean chocolate 26, 27
single-origin chocolate 26, 27
single-origin milk chocolate 29
single-plantation chocolate 27
smooshed bar 97
Snickers® 83, 99
spikes, chocolate 114
spirals, chocolate 114
Staite, Prudence Emma 128–9
stevia 18–19, 32
sugar in chocolate 18
adding 25
alterative-sugar chocolate 32
sugar and spice cocoa nib
kisses 65
'Sweet Like Chocolate' (Shanks
and Bigfoot) 126–7
sweetening chocolate 18–19, 62

T

tart, chocolate 109, 155, 202–4
tasting chocolate 38–49
with colour 41–2
emotional tasting 42
holding your own chocolate
tasting 44–5
slowing down 39–40
tannins 40
temperature 41

Valrhona tasting guide 42–3
see also eating chocolate
television adverts 78–81
tempered chocolate
balloon bowls 106
crumpled chocolate 109
dark chocolate truffles 49,
154, 164–5
shards 112
working with 105
wrapping a cake 105
tempering chocolate 25, 62–3
terminology 26–7
theobromine 18
Tijen 145–6
torte, chocolate truffle 154, 180
transfer sheets 111
Trinitario beans 16–17
triple-chocolate sandwich
cookies 154, 166–8
truffles 49
100 per cent dark chocolate
sugar-free vegan
truffles 155, 194
Kylie's chocolate 131
water ganache truffles 75
types of chocolate 27–33

V

Valrhona tasting guide 42–3
Vanillin 28
vegan milk (mylk)
chocolate 29–30
vegan truffles 155, 194
vegelate 82

W

White Aura Holistic Healing
145
white chocolate 28
modelling paste 110
White, Marco Pierre 78, 94, 121
*Willy Wonka and the Chocolate
Factory* 118–20, 140
wrappers 58, 150

Acknowledgements

I would like to thank Joanna Copestick, Louise McKeever, Judith Hannam and everyone at Kyle Books for believing in my vision for this wonderfully colourful and joyful book. Thank you to Tara O'Sullivan my amazing editor, who beautifully brought my words together. A special thank you to a dream team of creatives that brought this book to life: photographer Louise Hagger, designer Clare Skeats, food stylist Saskia Sidey and prop stylist Jennifer Kay. To my agent Borra Garson and Louise Leftwich, thank you for dreaming big with me. For his patience and support while writing this book, thank you to my wonderful partner Luke. Thanks also go to my business partner and all our team at paul a. young fine chocolates. To all the cacao farmers, chocolate producers, bean-to-bar makers and suppliers: without you, we would not have this wonderful industry and all the amazing chocolate. To all the contributors who helped bring my book alive with their talent, skill and generosity – thank you.

To all the cacao farmers in the world, thank you. What you do brings so much joy to so many, and I will continue to strive to help make your place in our industry a happier and more profitable one.

The challenges and difficulties that many farmers face across the globe are always at the forefront of my mind, and especially in regions like the Ivory Coast and Ghana, where there are still some acute issues with child trafficking, forced labour and farmers not being paid honestly and fairly. So much good work is being done by so many chocolate businesses to support farmers; however, we still have some serious issues within the industry. We can all help make a difference by supporting growers with the decisions we make when buying our chocolate, and doing a bit of homework about what we choose to buy. I will continue to support our growers wherever and whenever I can, either by buying chocolate direct from the producer who buys their beans from the grower, or by buying direct from the grower who also makes their beans into chocolate. It's going to be an ongoing challenge, and I hope the multinational chocolate companies who influence our industry and the ways in which consumers buy chocolate will make some significant and daring decisions in the coming years to make the entire chocolate industry a joy for everyone.